the smiths

THE COMPLETE STORY

KT-148-026

Omnibus Press
London/New York/Sydney/Cologne

Edited by **Chris Charlesworth**
Art Direction by **Mike Bell**
Book designed by **Stylorouge**
Picture research by **Valerie Boyd** & **Mary McCartney**

ISBN: 0.7119.1427.3
Order No: OP 43389

Exclusive distributors:
Book Sales Limited,
8/9 Frith Street, London W1V 5TZ, UK.

Music Sales Corporation,
24 East 22nd Street, New York, NY 10010, USA.

Music Sales Pty Ltd
120 Rothschild Avenue, Rosebery, NSW 2018, Australia.

To the Music Trade only:
Music Sales Limited,
8/9 Frith Street, London W1V 5TZ, UK.

Picture credits:
E. Blyton (courtesy of Rough Trade Records): 95.
Andre Csillag: Front & back covers, 99 (tx2), 109 (centre) and 114.
Kevin Cummins: 105 (bl), 110, 111 (t), 116 and 120 (b).
Joelle Depot: 9, 22, 23, 42, 64, 69, 81, 91 and 92.
London Features International: 3, 4, 6, 7, 15, 35, 40, 52, 53, 54, 56, 60,
62, 66, 68, 85, 96 (t), 98, 100, 101 (b), 102 (t&b), 108 (b), 122 and 124 (t).
Jo Novark (courtesy of Rough Trade Records); 97 (t&b), 99 (centre),
101 (t), 104, 105 (t), 107 (centre & b), 109 (b), 113, 115, 116 (insets), 117,
118, 120 (tl&tr) and 121.
Barry Plummer: 10, 14, 19, 40 (t), 49, 55, 58 (l), 60, 74, 83, 86, 88,
111 (b) and 112 (r).
Rex Features: 96 (b), 99 (b), 105 (br) and 107 (t).
Rough Trade: 103, 116 (t&b), 108 (t), 112 (l), 118 (b), 119, 123
and 124 (l).
Paul Slattery: 5, 8, 11, 12, 13, 16, 17, 18, 20, 21, 24, 25, 26, 27, 28, 29, 30,
31, 32, 33, 34, 38, 39, 40 (centre), 41, 43, 44, 45, 46, 47, 48, 50, 51, 56 (l),
57, 58 (r), 59, 61, 63, 65, 67, 70, 71, 72, 73, 75, 76, 77, 78, 79, 80, 82, 84,
87, 89, 90 and 94.
Typeset by floppy disc transfer by Capital Setters, London.
Printed in England by Wm. Clowes Limited, Beccles, Suffolk.

foreword

Today's pop music, an easily accessible and much needed form of escapism, offers very little that is worthy of comment and exploration. Record companies stamp an obvious seal on the face of any musical package before it even reaches our television screens or record decks. This 'shock tactic' approach, the product of financial panicking, makes for neat, 'safe', lightweight entertainment.

The Smiths fit neatly into this strategy as the exception to the rule. That The Smiths dismiss the all important mediums of video fashion and Fairlight affected pulsebeat, yet maintain their status as an immensely successful chart band, is itself a feat worthy of praise. This 'outsider' stance is, of course, nothing new, and if it bore the bulk of the band's appeal, would be nothing more than a gimmick in itself. The Smiths, however, run far deeper.

The articulate lyricism of Morrissey mirrors an entire lifestyle, and in so doing offers a constructive and plausible alternative way of thinking. Intelligent and well researched, Morrissey escapes the naivety and hypocrisy that has brought a thousand young and earnest rock stars before him into the shallow waters of the plastic art form pop music so often is. The past eight years has seen a steady and clever manipulation of the so-called thinking minority: the wheezes and schemes of cheeky pop entrepreneurs like Morley and McLaren have been championed in the rock press and elsewhere as a perfect parallel to the upwardly mobile mentality of the calculator and computer generation, the complete full circle from sixties hippiedom.

The Smiths run directly against the grain. They are far from perfect: a gulf appears naturally between their original ideals and their new found pedestal. They slip into inaccessible elitism. An inescapable irony. How the consequences of this situation are dealt with, by both band and fans, is dealt with quite openly within this book.

Far from being the obligatory rock biography (I believe such an account would be demeaning to both group and fans), this book is an attempt to discover the basis of a communication phenomenon. The Smiths. It is a measure of success, not in the commercial sense of the word but an exploration into just why The Smiths connect with so many and whether that connection invokes a solid and lasting influence or is simply a mere fad. It is also, merely, the story of a pop group but viewed through a wide angle lens. The facts and figures certainly lie underneath but, hopefully, they will prove to be the most unimportant part of the document.

STEVEN MORRISSEY'S
MANCHESTER.

1977. The Electric Circus. Collyhurst Street. Manchester.
Punk Sundays. The North's answer to London's
Roxy. A swirling vortex of low art, madness, mediocrity and,
occasionally, brilliance. A beautiful social breakaway from
the strict bouncer dominated norm of the suit and tie disco.
A prevailing sense of relief and a chance for everyone to
forge a career non-reliant on academic achievement. Pop
groups, writers, poets, photographers, promoters, sound
engineers and A & R men. All would-be's stunned by the
sudden realisation that they 'could be'. All basking in instant
Bohemia. Talent would determine the longevity but nobody
worried. The crazy party lifted Sundays up and out of the
traditional gloom. Another first. Swear, spit, dance, drink,
kiss. Touch illegal substances, touch people. The myth of
punk comradeship provided the sense of fun but, in essence,
it was little different to theatre cocktail parties. The Chablis
gave way to Newcastle Brown. Etiquette became
debauchery but opportunism still fuelled the conversation.

Expense account record company employees greedily
surveyed the proceedings from the bar. Lowering their
manners, they fell into the patronising pretence of dole-queue
banter. The best (Buzzcocks) and the worst (The Worst)
swapped their pint pots for amplifiers and partied onstage.
Between these two extremes a mass of erratic talent clambered
on to the boards, copied Johnny Rotten, delivered sixth-form
poetry, threw the bottles back and accepted the spittle. For a
short while (three months) the family party remained within
the crumbling Electric Circus walls but the talented and the
lucky soon matured into pop stars and ambitious writers. No
longer would it be possible to travel home on the bus with
your favourite artiste. As those deft enough left the circle the
remaining masses lost the sense of happening and re-entered
the obscurity of mundane reality. Bitterness, frustration and
jealousy crept slowly in and only proud bar room nostalgia
("I remember one night when me and Pete Shelley got pissed
and spent the night in Piccadilly Gardens...") remained.

Steven Patrick Morrissey was the ultimate embodiment of those left behind. In many respects, he still is. Steven Morrissey was a bar room intellectual and a New York Dolls fan. A year earlier he witnessed the Sex Pistols debacle at The Lesser Free Trade Hall, Manchester, a legendary bombastic event bludgeoned into rock history books by the Pistols' typical blind arrogance and contrived but constructive chaos. Steven Morrissey was impressed and compared the Pistols to his beloved New York Dolls in the *New Musical Express* letters page. "The Sex Pistols", he wrote, "are very New York and it's nice to see that the British have produced a band capable of producing the atmosphere created by The New York Dolls and their many imitators, even though it might be too late…"

By mid 1977, Morrissey's letter writing had already climbed into local notoriety. A fellow fanzine writer, Steve Shy from 'Shy Talk' (such were the ridiculous pseudonyms of the era) told me one typical Sunday…

"God, I've got another letter from that kid in Stretford. He's beginning to be a real pain. I'd like to write back but I can't keep up with him. He sent me a review of The Heartbreakers and maybe I'll print it…I don't know though…He goes on a bit…"

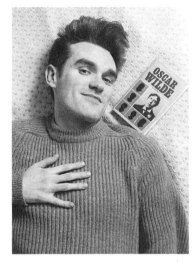

The Heartbreakers, formed from the sad dying fag end of the dirt/glam New York Dolls, were Johnny Thunders' short-haired vision of British punk. Not surprisingly, their most fanatical fan happened to be Steven Morrissey. He was to be found lurking in the band's dressing room whenever they ventured into Mancunian territory, which was often. The Heartbreakers were to fall from grace with violent rapidity towards the end of 1977, only to re-emerge as cult heroes in 1984. It's interesting to note that, a heavily guitar based sound apart, the gap between The Heartbreakers and The Smiths couldn't possibly be wider. Indeed, in retrospect, it is difficult to see just why the young Morrissey was drawn towards the New York Dolls school of hammy glitter at all. Their method of self parody and street clichés – the truly uninhabitable world of the drug crazed rock 'n' roll dream – seems perversely opposed to the lifestyle and set of beliefs that Steven Morrissey would later bring into the world.

Steven Morrissey was an armchair rebel during 1977. From his bedroom he communicated with the rest of the world through the power of the postage stamp. "The biggest crisis of my life came when the postal rate went up," he would later state, and only half in jest.

Steven thrived on the 'outsider' syndrome. His love of Oscar Wilde and James Dean verged on absolute fanaticism. His research was an unstoppable quest inspired by a fascination with those who lived by their own rules and nurtured a mistrust of the tactics of indoctrination. Indeed, Steven Morrissey was a rock 'n' roller in the purest sense of the phrase. The Art he loved, be it musical, cinematic or literature, was art which *just* stretched outside the boundaries of normality. Undeniably naïve, he nonetheless loved the magic which was beyond the grasp of record companies.

Far from the image of the shrinking wimp, Steven Morrissey was a model athlete at school, a running champion. Only this managed to save him from the bullying which would visit a boy who practically lived within the works of Oscar Wilde. (Wilde was introduced to him by his mother, a librarian, who couldn't possibly have anticipated the effect and, apparently, never regretted it even in the seemingly hopeless pre-Smiths days of unemployment and complete lack of desire to become gainfully employed.)

Steven Morrissey also loved record shops. From a very early age he hung around these mystical temples to 'smell the vinyl'. He studied record sleeves, watched the cash sales. What little money he did have was spent on a record selected with extreme care which became, to his way of thinking, a possession close to his heart. Even at the early teenage, Morrissey's sense of value was completely individual: naïve, eccentric, ingenious, illogical or exceptional, probably all of these and more. One wonders what would have become of Steven Morrissey if fate hadn't dealt him his measure of success. One wonders how many other Steven Morrisseys there are still sitting in their bedrooms. One scans the selling power of The Smiths and begins to realise the answer.

Steven Patrick Morrissey was born on the 22nd May 1959. By the age of ten he had taken to dreamily wandering around areas of Stretford and Hulme not normally reserved for the vision of one so young. He felt an early affinity with the plight of the local people. He adored *Coronation Street* so much that he wrote mock scripts for the show and began a correspondence with the show's producer Leslie Duxberry. His first record purchase, significantly, was Marianne Faithfull's 'Come And Stay With Me'.

He was placed at St. Mary's Secondary Modern, Stretford. He joined the Mott The Hoople fan club and spent most of his homework time addressing letters to that organisation. At thirteen he went (with, it seems, the entire youth of Manchester) to see T. Rex at Belle Vue Kings Hall. In 1975, he fell on to the dole queue. He began to etch into local notoriety via a series of small ads in the music press seeking to swap info with fellow New York Dolls fans.

The finest example of punk Manchester in 1977, forever unique in rock's poor travesty, was Buzzcocks and, in particular, their leader Pete Shelley. Shelley sold tender love songs to an audience hell bent on destruction and revenge. Shelley wore flares. Shelley wore suits pinned with a carnation. Shelley was inoffensive, human, honest, humble and subsequently far more dangerous than the pathetic macho world of the Joe Strummers who inhabited punk's general stance. Shelley skilfully created a method of pop lyricism which, basking in intelligence, not only connected with the punk hardcore and the hip-intellects but also the young, lightweight Top Of The Pops viewers. Pete Shelley achieved the impossible.

Steven Morrissey watched Pete Shelley. Steven Morrissey also watched Mark E. Smith. Fronting the ramshackle The Fall, Mark E. Smith used an uncompromising vocal attack to inflict a brutally unconventional view of life on the unsuspecting souls at the front of the audience. Sounds familiar? Maybe, but Mark E. Smith had the back-up knowledge to defeat any oncoming verbal attack from journalist or punter. Mark E. Smith knew what he was talking about. Like Shelley, he was a rarity. Like Shelley he was a lasting influence on Steven Morrissey. The fact that Smith was utterly and proudly northern and that The Fall always encapsulated a northern way of life has led to heavily denied speculation that The Smiths took their name from young Mark. This isn't important but the similarities in the aesthetic natures of the two bands remains blatantly obvious.

The Electric Circus closed down, due to ridiculous licensing laws, in October 1977. Manchester died a little and Morrissey retreated to the bedroom typewriter to produce two books. Firstly, and not surprisingly, there was a biography of The New York Dolls (he had begun to run The New York Dolls fan club), then a strange existential affair entitled 'James Dean Is Dead' which dealt with his hero's problems with the spoils of success. Both are out of print and according to his publisher (the wacky John Muir of Todmorden) are unlikely to see the light of day ever again.

"Morrissey had a wonderful twist of phrase", says Muir today, "His writing was really witty...really very clever but I found his personality fascinating which is why I decided to publish."

In 1979 Manchester television personality extraordinaire Tony Wilson scraped enough money together to start Factory Records and open the Factory Club in Hulme, consequently rejuvenating the Manchester rock scene. It was the period which spawned Joy Division, The Distractions, A Certain Ratio and Steven Morrissey's favourite Ludus. Despite being in the centre of the notorious inner-city area of Manchester (Hulme – an architectural tragedy born out of the fevered brain of a drawing board

moron and giving (high) rise to a staggering suicide rate. Factory loved to exploit, with sympathy, the grey feel of the area). The Factory Club had an easy going atmosphere which conformed to the decidedly 'arty' mood of the day. Friday nights became the new vortex of Mancunian activity and all four would-be Smiths spent time there.

Steven Morrissey used the evenings to try to break into rock journalism. He sent reviews to *Record Mirror* (occasionally under the nom-de-plume Sheridan Whitehead) and the *NME* but achieved little success. He was actually turned down five times by *NME* and this had a lasting effect: frustration and perhaps a desire to avenge himself in its columns in later years. Lack of attention aside, his name still cropped up in many conversations but he was never in any real danger of being taken seriously within the circle of Manchester's low art dwellers. Although always in the background he never managed – and probably had no desire – to join the hip elite of The Factory. He was, however, drawn towards Ludus and became friendly with their singer, songwriter, artist and leader, Linder.

Formed by the enigmatic Arthur Kadmon, Ludus became a vehicle for Linder's obscure and often unintelligible feminist lyrical and visual montages. A strange band, they rode a jazzy musical offshoot which often bordered on directionless experimentalism. They were interesting rather than entertaining and yet, to this day, remain Morrissey's favourite band. Linder, previously famous for designing Magazine album sleeves and working on montage projects with *Sounds* writer Jon Savage, slowly wrenched the group away from the ideas of Kadmon. Kadmon left to be replaced by Ian Devine. At this point, Steven Morrissey's friendship with Linder verged on infatuation and he moved into the flat she shared with Ian Devine. He stayed for a year and grew deeply interested in Linder's studious attitude towards feminist principles. He read continuously and nurtured a relationship which, by all accounts, verged on the 'extremely weird'. It is interesting to note that Ludas's then manager, Richard Boon (former Buzzcocks manager and 'New Hormones' supremo) was later to move to Rough Trade and become instrumental in the signing of The Smiths.

The Factory period intensified with the success of Joy Division and the astonishing failure of The Distractions. Bands flocked to the bedsits of Whalley Range and Didsbury. The feel was "Get to Manchester and get signed" although it rarely worked that way. One such band, Victim, made the break from their native Belfast and fell into a false sense of security by capturing a small time record contract with Tony Davidson's T.J.M. Label. They came for glory and found themselves huddled together in the smallest of Whalley Range bedsits. Whalley Range was, and still is, an intensely Bohemian area packed solid with aspiring and struggling bands. What these hopefuls achieved for their pleasure and pain was a violent lifestyle of abject poverty. The vision of bedsit freedom would soon turn sour. Morrissey was already writing songs about Whalley Range.

Victim released two singles, 'Strange Thing By Night' and 'Why Are Fire Engines Red'. In Belfast they achieved minor fame (on their bedroom wall a poster proudly displayed a Belfast Victim gig with support band The Undertones) but in Manchester they slipped away into the endless dull circle of local pub gigs. They had an English drummer by the name of Mike Joyce. His future success as one quarter of The Smiths must have seemed an impossible dream in those days. The plight of the aptly named Victim and hundreds like them wasn't enough to deter Steven Morrissey into a search for everyday employment. Later, he would tell Radio One's Janice Long: "I believed that I had my own work to do. I would rather starve than work for somebody else. I would gladly die in defence of that statement."

But Steven Morrissey's Manchester was rooted far deeper than the élitist circle of local rock music. Forever a romantic, and sometimes painfully so, he stayed true to his belief that he was "the last remaining cog in the Arndale Centre" (Manchester's hideous shopping centre). He believed in the legacy left from the industrial North and still felt the pain from an era when entire generations existed purely around the workings of the local mill, an age typified by Wakes week, where entire towns would holiday together in Blackpool. (When the mill closed for the summer break, the town would also close for the summer break).

This restricted freedom revolted Steven Morrissey, and his passion turned to the sixties when the 'George Best set' particularly liberated the city by proving that escapism is there for all who had eyes enough to avoid entrapment. That sixties period and all the stories from the era were to play a massive role in Morrissey's subsequent lyricism and his handling of The Smiths record sleeves: the stories, the Moors murders, Viv (Spend, Spend, Spend) Nicholson, Elsie Tanner (the perfect Northern character so desperately attempting to escape to a better lifestyle), the

stream of sixties Northern imagery films (from *The Family Way* through *Saturday Night And Sunday Morning* to *The Lovers*) and the countless left-overs from the Merseybeat era now parading their former moments of glory around working men's clubs. Such rainy visions formed the basis of Morrissey's songwriting, coupled with a fear that around the corner, the North of England faced even darker days.

Later, in June 1984, he spoke of Oscar Wilde and James Dean in a similar light: "James Dean, even though he was making enormous strides forward with his craft, was still incredibly miserable and obviously doomed. Which is exactly the quality Oscar Wilde had. That kind of mystical knowledge that there is something incredibly black around the corner. People who feel that way are quite special and always end up in a mangled mess." (*Smash Hits*. June 1984.)

Without a shadow of a doubt Steven Morrissey always saw himself in that light. That's not to say he aspired to being something of a genius himself, it's just that he felt a tremendous affinity with those people. Although Steven Morrissey's general depression, disgust and horror was certainly fuel for his songwriting (he wrote constantly, almost as if in anticipation of the forthcoming band), he never really thought to question why he wrote. "It's like saying why do you breathe?", he said.

There is certainly no evidence that Steven Morrissey ever considered himself capable of fronting a band in these wilderness years. He knew he wanted to write but just what medium he would use to convey his feelings was unclear. His strangely unsuccessful and continuing quest to write for music papers suggests he was seeking a career in some form of journalism.

Flushed with the phenomenal success of Joy Division/New Order, Factory Records opened The Haçienda club in May 1982. Intended as a kind of hip cathedral for the Manchester music scene, The Haçienda was the complete antithesis of The Electric Circus. Far from being a symbol of decay, it was a symbol of prosperity. The 'moderne designer' appearance combined with light 'Factory grey' paintwork to give an airy, cold ambience. Forever the purveyors of the super hip, Factory attracted a crowd 'too cool' to outwardly show any emotion. In no time at all, The Haçienda found itself with a reputation of being the coldest, most unresponsive, most apathetic gigging hall in the country. Factory greyness had dulled the senses and while the club was still the place to be, it certainly wasn't the place to play.

It is no secret that Steven Morrissey detested the overbearing coolness of The Haçienda. The lack of humanity, the emotionless sterility, were to become

Morrissey's main motivation in showering the place with flowers a little over a year later.

Summer 1982 and still Steven Morrissey remained in the shadows. Pop music was going through an unusually bright period as the *NME* mentality turned chartwards and championed such acts as ABC, Haircut One Hundred and even Dollar. Every sockless wonder in town partied to the lush tones of Trevor Horn's 'Lexicon of Love', and Morrissey found a purpose and humanity in Manchester's ideal packed but far from illustrious Secret Seven (a kind of heavy Dollar formed from the ashes of The Distractions and riding on a wave of hype).

In September '82, guitarist Johnny Marr was growing steadily tired of thrashing about on his own. He'd spent years tied to drum machines and Portostudios, crafting songwriting ideas but without finding the perfect format of presentation. He'd played with a few friends over the years but never managed to overcome the logistics of forming and fronting a band. His existence had been particularly dull, holding down brief part-time work selling clothes in Manchester's underground fashion world. He was searching for a complete lyricist who could add flavour to songs he was intending to be covered by bigger artists. He found Steven Morrissey.

It was through a friend who knew Morrissey five years previously and, although he hadn't seen him since, knew that he was still a prominent writer. Johnny Marr became interested. He'd heard weird stories of Steven Morrissey's unconventional approach to life.

Johnny Marr went round to Morrissey's house, rang the bell, pressed his nose against the window and left a large chocolate stain which niggled the answering Steven Morrissey. Johnny Marr was nervous. He thought Morrissey might think he looked too weird. (Marr was sporting a huge rockabilly quiff which looked like a French loaf sticking out of the top of his head.) All Marr really knew was that Morrissey had written a book about The New York Dolls and was quite prepared to spend the next hour talking about them if nothing else was to stem from the meeting. But as the bemused Morrissey answered the door Johnny Marr's tongue went into overdrive. He told Morrissey (the 'Steven' is dropped from this moment onwards) that this was how Leiber and Stoller had met. Morrissey let him in. Marr never stopped talking and enthusing and within an hour they were already writing songs together. It was the most important day in both their lives although at this stage all they considered was writing songs for other performers.

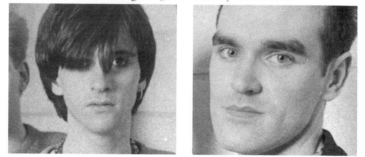

But they kept in constant touch. One of the first lyrics that Morrissey handed over to Marr was 'Suffer Little Children'. Written after Morrissey had read the chilling Beyond Belief, 'Suffer Little Children' was a deeply sensitive insight into the Moors Murders, a completely taboo subject in the streets of Manchester.

Marr was overwhelmed by the bravery of the lyric and the immensely humane way in which Morrissey tackled the subject. It triggered Marr into writing one of his most elegantly moody melodies to date. Slowly it began to dawn on the pair that nobody else could possibly represent their work. They developed a tremendous belief in their own capabilities and the partnership swiftly developed into an obsessive quest. Despite the jealous taunts from their friends and counterparts, Marr and Morrissey knew that something lasting had begun.

two

"The Devil will find work
for idle hands to do".

(from 'What Difference Does It Make'.)

It is, indeed, a rarity when initial enthusiastic ideas, plans, ideals and logistics fall into place with almost absolute perfection. Talent plays but a small part in the proceedings. Almost all successful and substantial talents spend years in reassessment, reorganization and the bewilderment of impending failure before fate deals a sideways measure of success which invariably comes from the direction of least expectation. Only a fool would believe the lie of, say, McLaren's 'Great Rock and Roll Swindle'. The Sex Pistols apparently instant recognition was in direct contrast to their original plan to build a new Bay City Rollers. Those who taste instant success usually falter quickly in the aftermath of their luck.

Morrissey and Marr made plans to become the most important British musical force since The Sex Pistols. The intensity of their relationship created a partnership of seemingly unstoppable solidity. But every aspiring new band in the country also held a belief in their own importance, talented and untalented alike. The stupidity of the British A & R system made sure that talent, genuine talent, became the most unimportant factor in initial returns.

"There is a buzz going around that I'm starting a band," quoth Morrissey and no one could blame his Mancunian counterparts for deliberately yawning at the suggestion. This unimposing fellow, who had failed at every stage so far, is starting a band? The cynics, licking their lips in anticipation, were ready and willing to use what little influence they had to keep this Morrissey thing under wraps. Johnny Marr was only an unknown beginner.

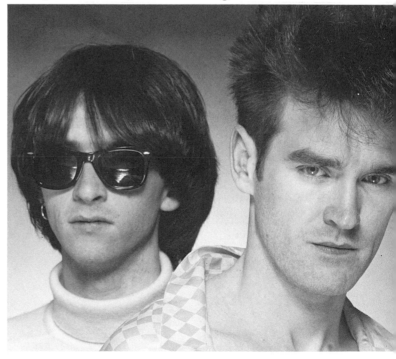

Morrissey and Marr borrowed a drummer and a few pounds and worked a night session in a scruffy Manchester 8-track studio. They managed to get down two songs, 'The Hand That Rocks The Cradle' and 'Suffer Little Children'. Johnny Marr played both guitar and bass. The session was ramshackled by inexpertise (remember, Morrissey hadn't sung before and to this day he remains a non-singer. This is fine when reputation and success back up your presence but, as an unknown, it is virtually certain to test the nerves of any recording engineer. Recording studios can be extremely embarrassing places). The two songs were played back the next day by the tired twosome. It was 'Suffer Little Children' which impressed the most. Johnny Marr couldn't believe the beauty of Morrissey's voice. Previously they had the conviction and the confidence but this tape was the final proof, the confirmation of the possibilities. Time and time again they listened to the tape. Their confidence grew into overwhelming proportions and in the opinion of many observers they swiftly became Manchester's tedious twosome. The tactic now was to convert and confirm.

Johnny Marr set about moulding a band around the songwriting. He phoned an old school friend named Andy Rourke. He hadn't seen him for years but knew of his bass playing. A meeting was arranged and Rourke, impressed by the tape, threw all his enthusiasm into the audition. The results are now obvious. A friend told Marr about Mike Joyce and his history in Victim and the punk outfit The Hoax. With amazing simplicity the foursome was complete. All of which may appear to be fairly straightforward, but to connect four musicians in such a short time with a combined objective and musical compatibility is no mean feat. Whether Morrissey and Marr realise the degree of luck involved is still subject to some speculation, for the combination was of four very diverse musical influences. Morrissey had a passion for sixties British pop, Dusty Springfield, Sandie Shaw. Marr shared these views but held more affinity with the American market of the same era, The Byrds, Martha Reeves and James Brown, Andy Rourke's listening was confined to Joni Mitchell, Dylan and Neil Young while Mike Joyce was still firmly stuck in The Undertones side of showbiz punk. It was an odd foursome indeed but rehearsals at Manchester's Twilight Studios went incredibly well and a live set was swiftly formulated. Marr's years spent in isolated songwriting obviously combined with Morrissey's lyrical backlog.

Their first gig was set at the Manchester Ritz, supporting the hyped Blue Rondo A La Turk on October 4th 1982. The band approached the event with some trepidation. Firstly, The Ritz isn't an ordinary début gig club. Large and cavernous, The Ritz is a genuine twenties dancehall which once played host to all the giants of the jazz era. In 1982 it began to challenge The Haçienda as the alternative modern performance hall. Strangely, The Ritz attracted a punkier, rowdier crowd altogether. Secondly, Blue Rondo represented everything that the newly constituted foursome had pledged to hate. Blue Rondo was the instant vision of a marketing campaign. Hip to the cocktail circuit, they had used their many contacts to construct a massive hype, especially in the fashion press. Blue Rondo was fast realising that British youth could not be moulded from lentil burger gorged bodies in Covent Garden offices. That said, they did attract an audience decked out in all the cool of high fashion.

One day, as Johnny Marr sat patiently in Morrissey's flat, Morrissey produced a large piece of card with the words 'The Smiths' scratched across. Morrissey didn't produce it necessarily as a potential name for the foursome but Marr's reaction was ecstatic. Together they allowed their enthusiasm to formulate seemingly perfect reasons to be called The Smiths.

"All other bands at the time had fifteen syllable names", says Marr. "It was like, well, these groups have all got together and thought 'Well, we'll get these haircuts and these clothes and it will give us a concept that people can grab hold on to straight away'. We thought that that made the members of the bands faceless. We just wanted four individuals who could be collectively known as something normal. Smith is the most common name in the universe. It is inoffensive. I think at first it seemed to work at a disadvantage. Reviewers would put 'When I first heard the name I expected four guys in Factory haircuts'. I could understand that and was delighted when I saw people realising that we most certainly were not steeped in Factory greyness."

Their talent for self-promotion ensured that many people turned up at The Ritz to witness the intriguing spectacle of The Smiths falling on their collective backsides. This wasn't to be, although the gig was hardly lacking in mini disasters. The ridiculous Blue Rondo adopted a typical superstar approach and soundcheck time was kept at a minimum for the green and scruffy Mancunians. The situation did not improve when Morrissey was told that he couldn't alter the height of the mikestand. The debuting vocalist therefore spent the entire set stooping to sing through a microphone a foot shorter than his requirement, hardly a sure-fire confidence booster. They stumbled through, relying on practice room unity and the simplicity of their classical rock band format to ease the atrocious sound problems.

Their reception was middling but this was a major triumph. The band's resolve increased tenfold, although Morrissey was a little stunned by the enormity of his upcoming task. Nobody, however, laughed at Morrissey's pretensions. Equally though, nobody could possibly visualise the meteoric rise that lay ahead.

In Manchester, and possibly elsewhere, 1983 belonged well and truly to New Order. The monumental 'Blue Monday' became (arguably) the biggest selling record of the year. Certainly it was the largest grossing twelve inch of all time, moving Factory Records into worldwide markets they never even dreamed of reaching. As far as The Smiths were concerned the importance of this success cannot be underestimated. 'Blue Monday', hypnotic and unrelenting, was the product of New Order's electronic naïvety, encouraging a simplicity and humanity within the workings of the highly technical disco market. New Order were proving they could compete with the largely faceless and bland disco outpourings of the major corporations, and also that it was possible to channel their personal intensity through this format. As the Factory supremo Tony Wilson pointed out at the time, "New Order are leading us into an age of passionate computer music". The all important hip-consciousness of Manchester wholeheartedly jerked to the harsh snap of the Linn Drum.

The Smiths, with their traditional bass/drums/guitar set up, were in grave danger of sounding out-moded while still in the embryonic stage. There seemed little point in worrying; the 12-string guitar work of Johnny Marr was to play a crucial part in the band's make up. Thankfully, Tony Wilson was wrong. As with all so-called movements, an anti-movement is created instantaneously by the same audience. Marr and Morrissey believed in a certain purity and honesty. They decided to forget all current trends (such young band paranoia, the decision to trend hop, often leads to directionless confusion anyway) and concentrate on keeping their music within the reach of their collective

ability. The Smiths couldn't be outmoded or old fashioned simply because they would be so different. This was their theory. (By 1983, fashion had become so disjointed anyway – it became possible to achieve the look and sound of any youth cult movement since the forties and still remain firmly in vogue).

Johnny Marr: "We never claimed to be fashionable, musically or clothes wise so we never cared. Personally I've always been into style and clothes though. The only job I've ever done was selling trendy clothes so I've got wardrobes full of them. I know as good as the next man what is hip but we decided to forget all that and just concentrate on good songs. Good songs are all that matter anyway."

Radio One's Janice Long: "Old fashioned? Never, The Smiths now make Duran Duran, Nik Kershaw or Michael Jackson look years out of date so how could they have been seen as old fashioned at the start? The Smiths make music. That actually means something – it's not frivolous – so consequently it can't be classed as, or even thought of as, old fashioned."

The Smith's reputation, their 'buzz', evolved steadily during 1983. Morrissey and Marr found songwriting easy and perfectly natural. Their second gig earned them a rave review by the *NME's* Jim Shelley. A splattering of gigs in London actually dragged the journalists that mattered out of their ivory towers.

"The songs…" wrote Johnny Waller in *Sounds*. "What an amazing collection of pop songs." This quote came after The Smiths had played that unfashionable London graveyard for provincial bands, The Rock Garden. In Manchester they played to twenty-five people at the now sadly defunct gay bar Manhattan Sound. "They seem to think they are something special", muttered one unimpressed observer. *Sounds*man Dave McCullouch took up The Smiths case. (Not necessarily a good thing as McCullouch, esoteric as always, often attached a McCullouch stigma to his favoured acts. The phrase 'A Dave McCullouch band' was often used to describe those whose musical wanderings took them into the world of personal art ethics and therefore obscurity.) But McCullouch had good ears and a sharp vision for aesthetic quality. It was McCullouch who first exploited Morrissey's vision born from the use of the words 'handsome' and 'charming'. Both words were used to push the Morrissey vision of men's liberation; not, as it may sound, a freedom given to the Penthouse reading hordes but a glimpse of Morrissey's ideal world where gender barriers are entirely dispensed with. When he was 14 he read a book entitled 'Men's Liberation' which dealt with aspects of sex segregation. Morrissey found it terrible that people were so rigidly divided, that men could only like men's things and women women's things.

Morrissey couldn't understand why people (men in particular) were terribly afraid of emotionalism. This hatred of accepted barriers was another throwback to his distaste for Victorian attitudes still practised in many Northern towns. Morrissey often felt unattractive and uncharming in his bedsit gloom. Liberation from this feeling, he felt, was simply a state of mind. Two songs 'This Charming Man' and 'Handsome Devil' were born out of these feelings as was his (soon to be much publicised) use of flowers. Suddenly, The Smiths had gained an image. Suddenly, they were playing the game.

Morrissey, in particular, found a second artistic release in his talent for dominating interviews. He made easy copy and journalists loved his accessibility. Their gig attendances grew at an alarming rate and occasional support spots to The Fall were no longer a viable notion. "So when are they going to sign to Factory?" came the cry, but a rebellious gig where the band showered The Hacienda with flowers virtually negated this particular course of action.

In came the A & R sheep. In came the clothes shop owning, rugby playing manager Joe Moss, and in came a traumatic realisation that bedsit jabbering and glorious friendships were not enough. The Smiths were about to become involved in hard business.

"In my life, Oh why do I give valuable time to people who I'd much rather kick in the eye?" (From 'William, It Was Really Nothing').

The sudden appearance of record company A & R men induces paranoia for any band. The sudden impact of being in a situation of which you have long dreamed is a temporary high, soon destroyed by the dread of the possibility of them all going away again. This is, however, just the beginning. In no time at all the record company boys will impose their vision on the band and how they think it should be marketed, and how fast, and to what audience, and with what producer, and what songs, and what should the press angle be? The Smiths,

between grabbing valuable demo time from interested companies, found themselves, in the long hot summer of '83, in the centre of a whirlwind of ideas all blossoming from the seeds of that initial Marr and Morrissey meeting less than one year earlier. It was indeed a difficult time. The temptation to let go was strongly compelling and had a good argument to back it up. Morrissey, Marr, Joyce, Rourke and Moss collectively worried about losing the chance of success. They talked to the record companies.

Johnny Marr: "We got offers from every major company in England and a few in America. It got like an auction. We had great fun going round seeing everybody and building up the bidding."

But Morrissey, speaking to *Melody Maker's* Ian Pye, later put a different slant on the meetings. "We felt out of place at every meeting. Our aims were not in line with theirs. Experiencing the majors was a pretty horrendous experience. They couldn't see beyond what had already sold."

Joe Moss ("A likeable chap with an enormous knowledge of rock music" – Dave McCullouch) took the band to Rough Trade where a much greater empathy seemed apparent.

Yet again The Smiths made a completely unfashionable choice. Rough Trade, once the darlings of the music press, had been cast aside as hopeless idealists when the major companies once more gained control of the market. The independent Rough Trade, with initial major distribution problems, had undeservedly been tagged as a testing ground for the bigger labels.

Johnny Marr: "It was a conscious decision to sign to Rough Trade because they had done a lot of good work in the past and right from day one they were our friends which is the most important thing. They knew that they needed us and it was a question of our integrity and our goodwill. We could have got lots of glossy pics in HMV and Virgin. But we thought the records would be good enough to happen without all that. We felt strongly enough to go with people who trusted us. The money was alluring but the people with the money were very unattractive. We thought we'd set an example. It's about time groups felt more about the music than the money."

The initial contract with Rough Trade was a simple singles deal. The company couldn't foresee great success or they would have tied the band up for years by way of contract options. Rough Trade ran the risk of losing The Smiths after creating the promotional success. The Smiths signed quickly to Rough Trade, a dangerous move, especially in the light of the the slobbering cheque book waving majors. But it was a brave move and a sign that the band held true to the courage of their convictions. Everyone wanted to know one thing. Who was this strange flower

waving fellow and what could the band possibly sound like?

That bastion of the up and coming English band, The John Peel Show, gave a welcome airing for the inquisitive hundreds. The Smiths recorded three John Peel sessions in the preceding months, comprising 'This Charming Man', 'Handsome Devil', 'Reel Around The Fountain', 'Back To The Old House', 'Still Ill', 'What Difference Does It Make' and 'This Night Has Opened My Eyes'. The response was tremendous and Peel constantly repeated the sessions. It was on one of those occasions that the power and diversity of night time Radio One managed to lift a band out of newspaper print and into the public's ears. Often slagged for its patronising attitude, Radio One, at its best, can create public demand before the record companies can touch a unit. The Smiths never forgot the debt they owed to John Peel and promised to repay, some day.

Although the band could now operate without digging into the personal pocket of Joe Moss (previously he had financed all the band's expenses), Marr, Morrissey, Rourke and Joyce still found themselves with little personal money. This was not such a bad thing at this stage. Morrissey's songwriting still stemmed from the angle of poverty and this early repertoire would last for eighteen months of success.

The Smiths, defying the trend of white electro beat, found themselves at the forefront of a new wave of 'pick up your guitar' bands. Such is the irony and stupidity of this fickle rock world. The Smiths, determined anti-bandwaggoners, had finally been pigeon holed. Retreating from press and other media distractions, they set about the search for the single. 'Reel Around The Fountain' (in its pre-controversy days) was the first choice and looked a certainty with its irresistible slowly bouncing melody until an instantly perfect 'Hand In Glove' changed minds and tactical manoeuvres.

"This is the most important song in the world," quoth Morrissey...extensively.

three

"The sun shines out
of our behinds".
(from 'Hand In Glove')

The most important song in the world was released in May 1983. Backed with 'Handsome Devil', it proved the perfect artifact to display the succinct yet overall perception of just what this strange new band was all about. Packaged in a disturbingly brave grey sleeve (depicting the rear regions of a naked angst ridden, shorn haired young man) it verged dangerously close to Factory's *moderne* Savilleion artwork. Many scorned it but rapturous press reviews helped push the record up into the high altitudes of the independent chart. For a while it looked like a possibility for national attention. Considering that this was a minor single on a label that, with respect, specialised in the production of minor singles, 'Hand In Glove' was, for all intents and purposes, a hit record. It was also the finest love song since Joy Division's 'Love Will Tear Us Apart'.

Without doubt, Johnny Marr managed to produce the perfectly weighted sliding rhythms to complement Morrissey's cynical lyricism. 'Hand In Glove', as if written in the euphoric condition of a new found love affair, holds all the ecstasy of that irrational condition with a typical defeatist twist in the tail. 'Hand In Glove' contained a determination only defeated by the writer's impending sense of doom. Sounds pretentious? Indeed, but it is a pretension which effectively connects with the masses. You can't argue with connection.

'Hand In Glove' put Morrissey on to the cover of everything. Once again The Smiths waltzed into a situation far in advance of their short-lived career.

Those live gigs became dangerously packed. Joe Moss's phone never stopped ringing. The press began to see Morrissey as the spokesman for a new generation.

orrissey took his flower fetish to extraordinary proportions. The band spent a fortune on chrysanthemums, employing people to distribute them at every gig. Still, it seemed, Morrissey's hatred of Factory greyness and his passion for old Oscar Wilde (also a flower addict) held true. It all became a little circus like. It also became easy to criticise. The Smiths were regarded by cynics as flower wimps. Anticipation of a press backlash ran high within the band. It was not to be. The Smiths were voted 'Best New Act' by the readership of the *NME*.

Morrissey was ecstatic at the response. His easy-going "I knew it would happen" stance belied his secret fears of "What if it all falls flat". He strongly denies this, of course, but who but a dedicated optimist could have so much

confidence? Morrissey armed himself with a self made shield of absolute and utter confidence. His stage presence improved dramatically. A non dancer by nature, he swirled around the stage in a glorious celebration of newly liberated frustration. Johnny Marr's guitar work may have been a stable basis of listenability but it was Morrissey's release from years of repressed loser attitudes which made The Smiths so special. Suddenly the one-off singles deal took on lengthier proportions and a second single was chosen from the pack.

One day, a charmingly hopeful advertisement adorned the doorway of a clothes shop in Stockport. Strangely enough the clothes shop had once been the home of Paul Morley who sat in residence in its previous existence as a secondhand book sellers. (Morley moved on to greater things as Britain's leading rock journalist and then even greater things as the mentor behind Frankie Goes To Hollywood).The clothes shop, named 'Crazy Face', was owned by a businessman hoping for greater things named Joe Moss. The people of Stockport couldn't give a damn.

Two weeks later The Smiths were on *Top Of The Pops*. There was Morrissey, the Whalley Range eccentric, the hopeless sender of a million hopeless letters, the weird kid from Stretford. There he was swirling a bunch of flowers, dressed in ill-fitting Levi's (surely Joe Moss could have fitted him out for the event) and a ridiculous shirt. There he was pledging the despair of a charming loser, the most unlikely rock star of all time. Throughout Manchester jaws dropped in disbelief. But if it was to be the first triumphant scream of Morrissey's revenge, then it was certainly a just reward for Johnny Marr. The Smiths were Morrissey's vehicle but they were Marr's baby and the guitarist relaxed with satisfaction at the rear of the set. The record only reached number twenty-five but the audience about to be touched was obviously going to be huge.

The Smiths preceded The Thompson Twins. It was one of those Thursdays. Despite their noticeable satisfaction, they looked decidely awkward. The 'whooping' dancers clashed violently with the band's deliberate down-market visuals. Only Morrissey looked the part, ensconced as he was in a wild celebration of his now successful madness. Just why 'This Charming Man' achieved the success denied to the stronger 'Hand In Glove' remains a mystery. The answer probably lies in the complex maze of hype, distribution, promotion and luck which makes up today's rock biz. As it happened, 'Hand In Glove' would soon seek glorious revenge anyway. The Smiths began to relish the success given to them by the lyrically obscure 'This Charming Man'. Did they enjoy Top Of The Pops?

Johnny Marr: "The first time we did Top Of The Pops it was quite horrible. The miming aspect of it was a drag but I was really glad to be on there to dispense with all those horrible people. Mind you, the Top Of The Pops we were on included The Alarm and Echo And The Bunnymen. Regardless of whether you like those groups or not, they are people with integrity. I like the fact that we sold enough records to go on there even if the event was a little embarrassing."

s Christmas 1983 neared, The Smiths made a lightning visit to America. Initially they planned a series of gigs but Mike Joyce fell ill and only a New York Danceteria date on New Year's Eve remained. Danceteria, a scruffy and confusing mess of three floors and an élitist rooftop, was the focal point of American trendiness. Whereas the bulk of America has been traditionally slow to latch on to new British acts, the more European attitudes of New York welcomed anything English and wielding a guitar. The success of 'The Face' in New York has brought the city parallel with London...and vice-versa. It has produced an overwhelming and fairly cultish New York knowledge of up and coming British bands. Needless to say, they were well primed for The Smiths.

The band caused a sensation on New Year's Eve, helping to produce, by all accounts, a classic evening. Joe Moss, however, was beginning to feel ill at ease as the rest of the band indulged in typical rock 'n' roll trappings that were at odds with Morrissey's stated philosophy. (The next visit to the States would intensify his annoyance and prove instrumental in his departure from the band). However, despite this and despite signing a lucrative deal in America with Sire, the band were not over impressed with the Americans.

Andy Rourke: "Sure we went down well but the buzz over there is quite staggering and they are still into all that 'noo wave' garbage. They see The Police or Duran as new wave. A week later they would be going mad for Def Leppard. All the bands who we slagged off when we were in England.''

Morrissey (to *Melody Maker, Sounds, Record Mirror* etc.): "We were asked to support The Police. How could we? We are far more important than The Police.''

Maybe it was the forthcoming U.S. date(s) that inspired them, maybe it was the smell of money but on December 10 Rough Trade made an error by issuing a New York dance mix version of 'This Charming Man'. The record, aptly renamed 'This Charming Man New York', was originally intended to be a DJ pressing only but Rough Trade changed their minds and issued the offending article nationally. It wasn't that the new treatment was particularly bad, it was just that the very idea of a re-mix fell directly against the grain of the code of ethics publicly laid down by The Smiths. Not surprisingly, and with good cause, the cries of "Sell out" went up all around the country. This was the first sign of weakness. It was O.K. for The Smiths to spout away with venom but when success beckoned would they be any different from anybody else? Many expressed doubt. Although the record initially had the band's approval, they soon changed tack when the implications were realised.

Morrissey would tell Janice Long: "Yeah, that record was our one flaw. A bad mistake and I'd agree with the critics but I suspect we can all be terribly sensible about it and forget all about it...please."

Not surprisingly this became the least selling Smiths record of them all. Both band and company quietly let the thing slip away, never to be mentioned again.

January 20 1984 saw the release of 'What Difference Does It Make.' Again the expected 'Reel Around The Fountain' single failed to materialise. 'What Difference...', always a single and a throwback to very early rehearsals, achieved instant recognition for being one of the shortest singles in history. A pocket of hardly welcome press pointed this fact out very clearly and certainly did little to mend the damage caused by the re-mix. The single was, however, speedy, hooky, catchy and the finest example of Morrissey's skilful warping of sentences to date. 'What Difference..' was packed with cynicism and hopelessness that reacted beautifully against the Morrissey ideology of a handsome and charming frame of mind. 'What Difference Does It Make?' was a catch phrase with a catch.

It was a statement on the futility of The Smiths art. It was another tender love song. It was all these things and more, whether Morrissey intended it to be or not. The song bounced along to reach the number twelve spot, helped by another uncomfortable but satisfying Top Of The Pops appearance and a fresh wave of publicity surrounding The Smiths affection for, and desire to, work with Sandie Shaw.

'What Difference Does It make' led the band neatly into their first major tour. Beginning at Sheffield University on January 31, the tour was to weave its way through nineteen (mainly university) dates before finishing triumphantly at Manchester's ultra-prestigious Free Trade Hall on February 13. Just seventeen months separated that lowly first supporting performance at The Ritz to headlining the city's most prestigious concert hall.

From the tour a distressing evening found its way on to TV screens. BBC2 filmed the Derby Assembly Rooms gig for inclusion in their Sight And Sound series. Transmitted at peak time Saturday evening, it presented The Smiths in a state of musical disarray. The sound was abysmal and the songs became submerged as the television company lost the age old battle to capture the live atmosphere. This said, the gig did finish with a mass stage invasion, another example of bands gathering an intensely fanatical following. The tour was appropriately chaotic, as most rock tours are: their first taste of the twenty-four hour a day, day to day flogging to which they would have to submit in order to compete. Days of casual romanticism were seemingly lost and the dark cliché-ridden existence of the typical 'on the road' band was, it appeared, the only possible future. Johnny Marr felt like Keith Richards. Johnny Marr began to wear sunglasses. This

was a dangerous sign. In a worse condition was Morrissey who fell victim to the gruelling schedule. A batch of dates on the tail end of the tour, chiefly in Scotland and Ireland, had to be cancelled as the singer struggled with flu, a lost voice and a frightening panic crisis. Would they burn out? Whatever, the intense press exposure showed no signs of letting up.

Morrissey made no new friends when reviewing the singles for *Record Mirror* on February 4 1984. With his by now legendary disregard for anything current which wasn't The Smiths or his personal protégé (the superb Easterhouse fell in his favour at this time), Morrissey performed ceremonial destruction with Sade, Style Council, Ultravox, Carmel, Genesis, Marilyn and, ironically enough, Blue Rondo who by this time were probably bragging about how The Smiths once supported them; poetic justic indeed. Morrissey makes a lousy rock critic though it is hard to disagree with his put-downs.

The obsessive and lightweight dismissals in *Record Mirror* hinted at a Morrissey who was beginning to live within his own self appraisal. While the humane and personal edge to his songwriting now connected with thousands, he faced the danger of creating an unlikeable monster blinded by defensive arrogance. Time would tell. Marr continously denied stories that he was becoming tired of the attention Morrissey received. "It would be childish to be jealous just because Morrissey holds the focal point," he said. "That was always the intention anyway. We are not in the business of becoming pop stars."

The Smiths most definitely were in the business of becoming pop stars. There was no truth in rumours of a group split.

Joyce and Rourke made no comment. Forever in the shadows, they were happy to progress as a rhythm section. Joyce and Rourke were just happy to have found a dream lifestyle though they occasionally questioned why their pockets were still empty. Johnny Marr simply clutched his twelve-string Rickenbacker (which once belonged to one of his heroes, Roger McGuinn from The Byrds) and concentrated on the meagre task of fulfilling the promise held by one of the most eagerly awaited début albums in history. Pending its release, Morrissey fell into convalescence back in Manchester, gently easing his voice back into shape at rehearsals in Twilight Studios. It was here that a friendly Johnny Marr, embarrassed by success, deliberately became a father figure to smaller local acts practising in the rooms next door. One band, Sense Of Purpose, expressed a desire to start a fanzine based around The Smiths. Marr was readily eager to prove his accessibility.

"Hey lads", he would shout as he pushed his head through the door. "Did I tell you about the cover from 'What Difference...'? That copy you've got, well it will be slightly rare because it has Terence Stamp on the cover. It was a still from a film called The Collector. (The film of the early John Fowles novel of the same name). Well, after we sold about fifty thousand, Terence Stamp decided that he didn't want to be on our cover so we got Morrissey to pose in the same position. From now on all the covers will be the mock-up version."

Marr, a genuinely helpful person, actually believed that such trivia would be vital information to young listening ears. Perhaps this was the case but there is a danger of becoming so immersed in oneself that the music tends to lose its relevancy. The Smiths have thus far managed to escape this trap but just how is a matter of some debate. Maybe this is the source of their unique appeal; whatever they may feel as individuals, they manage to continuously channel the music through completely humble observations. Such is the talent of Morrissey. Do you really want trivia? Here's a snippet: Johnny Marr's real name is John Maher but as that was the name of The Buzzcock's drummer, he changed to his present monicker.

The Smiths were, at this time, lying low and eagerly awaiting the release of the album. "I think it will be one of the great milestones in the history of pop. One of the most unforgettable events," said Marr.

four

The Album

"I think popular music is the last refuge of young people in the world. It's the only remaining art form. There's nothing else that touches them." (Morrissey speaking to Rob Graham from Manchester's *City Life* magazine.)

The album was originally to be called 'The Hand That Rocks The Cradle' but there was a last minute rethink at Rough Trade. Into the shops came 'The Smiths'.

he Smiths' wasn't the pop masterpiece it could have been; later, even the band recognised this fact. Those fanatics who taped John Peel sessions were disturbed by the album's lack of clarity. Although individually each song worked, when placed in a collective package the effect was a clouding of the impact. The songs fell together in a muddy pool of short-sighted production: not a bad début album by any standards but this was intended to be a complete signal post in the history of popular music. Frankly, there are moments where the album dips into the downright maudlin. The statement of light had become a depressing and, at times, boring mess of discontent. There were moments ('Reel Around The Fountain', 'Pretty Girls Make Graves' and the singles) which surpassed any music produced in 1984. The much publicised 'Suffer Little Children', however, failed to live up to expectations of pure beauty and honesty. The most annoying fact was that it could and should have been a masterpiece. The sleeve, a purple tint of yet another naked and desperate young man, did little but submerge the record further into dullness.

The music press didn't take the record and hail it to the Gods. Every review, though, finished safely along the

lines of, "They'll make the perfect album next time".

It became clear that The Smiths would escape with expectations for future brilliance still intact from every quarter. The perfect answer to all the music press critics: the massed armies of the anti-Morrissey brigade and yours truly (who bought the record only to give it away a week later after feeling let down), came by way of the fans. The album sold by the skip full and, production faults aside, Morrissey's sentiments still made that vital connection with the thinking patterns of the nation's youth. Many a bedroom door was tightly shut for six weeks while the inmate consumed and (that old cliché) related to the sentiments expressed. One hesitates to suggest that the huge majority of Smiths converts were male (this was to change quite dramatically later) and that the band had become a male vision, an ironic twist when considering the Morrissey hatred of gender divides. Were The Smiths to become an extension of that which Morrissey so detested? The circles seemed to be ever decreasing. There was a trap around every corner.

Then, the minor explosion.

The *Manchester Evening News* reported alleged complaints that 'Reel Around The Fountain' (by the 'controversial' pop group The Smiths) contained lyrics relating to child molesting. The national dailies loved this and immediately jumped on Morrissey's back in a typical display of hounding. I'm not going to dwell too deeply on this as I personally (and I know many people feel the same way) can't find one trace of child molestation or anything else distasteful within those grooves. Without doubt the gutter press whirlwind contained no substance whatsoever. This was the product of a search for a story whether the story was really there or not, and it was sufficient to cause ripples of pathetic hysteria. To be mercenary, this helped elevate The Smiths into national notoriety. The irony was that an episode which offered proof of Morrissey's distrust of established institutions now elevated The Smiths to an almost legendary status.

Morrissey didn't see it that way. Morrissey took the phone off the hook and retreated to a London flat. Morrissey refused to give interviews. In the North, people wondered why Morrissey took a flat in a fashionable area of London after he had openly pledged that he would never leave his home city. In Manchester this revelation caused many a disgruntled fan to spout off about pop stars and their separation from former values. "I'll never be considered a Southerner. I'll always be wandering around the North somewhere," Morrissey told *No. 1* magazine in March 1984.

Two months prior to making this statement Morrissey had moved to London (leaving the rest of the band a hundred and eighty miles up the motorway) to keep an eye on people. Living in London, he felt, was a necessity. He had no intention of letting another 'New York Mix' type blunder slip out through his lack of business suss. Morrissey was still very upset about that incident and wanted to be close to the decision makers. In a February issue of *Record Mirror* he displayed a strange coldness towards his leaving the band behind.

"Well, we are in daily contact", he said. "I don't feel that I have to gaze at their profiles or anything. They do get a bit jealous sometimes and I won't deny that they are not exactly ecstatic when another interview with me occurs".

So, apart from the odd practice session and a brief period recovering from illness, Morrissey was completely detached from Marr, Joyce and Rourke.

He was also completely detached from the rest of the world. Paranoid of the tabloids and their quest for story invention, Morrissey fell into the archetypal superstar lifestyle. The dailies would clock him every now and then, leaving his flat and cowering under a flash of camera light. Having lunch in Paris with Boy George? It seemed a long way from his flat in Whalley Range. Strange stories began to circulate about Morrissey's new residence. He had, according to rumour, a corner which was completely festooned with his own photographs; his own personal shrine, his own glorification of his new status. He sent a postcard to a well known photographer stating: "Your cover shot of me moved me enormously. I must have that picture. I must have it lifesize."

Was the man losing control? It was a difficult period warped by misquotes and media caricature. Morrissey's retreat was probably due to a realisation that he couldn't control his own public persona. It had become a creation of the press and not of himself. He had become two people. Now he decided to kill off the false one.

B ut other things happened within the music industry which effectively took the heat away from The Smiths in the early months of 1984. The nation had discovered Frankie Goes To Hollywood. Mike Read had discovered the sexual innuendo of 'Relax' and, by prescribing a Radio One ban, provided the catalyst for a media explosion. Embarrassingly for Read, 'Relax' rebounded to the number one spot and Frankie Goes To Hollywood became The Sex Pistols in pantomime. The tabloids sniffed money and fell into a frenzy. The resulting hype, which was to last six months, made the 'Reel Around The Fountain' accusations seem trivial by comparison. A strange looking band named Bronski Beat began to state a national case for gay equality. Sade became a ritzy superstar. Wham re-emerged as the new Bay City Rollers. Pop music had enough to concentrate on. It became easy for The Smiths to retain their true audience. The relentless electro-beat of the charts only improved their status as the main alternative.

five

Sandie Shaw

By April 1984 Morrissey and Marr's passion for the barefoot waif of the sixties had been well documented. To most the passion seemed oddly misplaced. Wasn't it the thing for newly made rock stars to pledge an allegiance to an old jazz hero, a John Coltrane, a Charlie Mingus or onwards into obscurity? Or a star from sixties soul, Otis Redding, James Brown, or Wilson Pickett? Or the film star crooning of a Sinatra, Peggy Lee, or Judy Garland? At the very least an average rock star could get away with Marc Bolan as his (or her) greatest hero.

British Merseybeat had always been a no-go era. Most recollections of Sandie Shaw stem no further than muddy images of television appearances in 1965 (or was that Cilla Black?) and her victory in that disturbing parody of an event, The Eurovision Song Contest. 'Puppet On A String' indeed.

But, as Morrissey was to point out, there was more to Sandie Shaw than that. Her packet full of 1965 hits,

'I'll Stop At Nothing', 'Long Live Love', 'Message Understood' and 'How Can You Tell', displayed a singer of some passion, a voice with the depth of soul far removed from the shrill chirpiness of Cilla Black or the bubbly fun-packed discotheque shouting of Lulu. Both were perfectly able media personalities, of course, but Sandie Shaw never seemed to fit into that Saturday evening family entertainment role. After Shaw hit her unfortunate pinnacle ('Puppet On A String'), she decided not to grow into desperate pantomime but discover the importance of real life as far away from the music business as possible. Sandie's true ambitions ran away from the desperate rat race and since then she had been content to dabble, treating her music as an entertaining sideline. This gave her a certain mystique: everyone wants fame, fame, fame and more fame, don't they? How could she desert the treadmill? Such drastic action was bound to invoke a certain cult appeal.

The best concise history of the singer was penned by Morrissey himself in the December 24 issue of *Sounds*. He wrote: "Without supernatural beauty, Sandie Shaw cut an unusual figure and would herald a new abandoned casualness for female singers. The grande dame gestures of the late fifties had gone, the overblown and icky sentiment had gone. In its place came a brashness and fortitude. Girls with extreme youth and high spirits were to boldly claim their patch in a business which was obviously a male domain."

Morrissey obviously saw young Sandie as a lead figure to herald a new age of feminism. Shaw, Black and Lulu all cheekily carved their own slices of the cake before they had reached the matronly age of eighteen.

The Smiths had wanted to work with Sandie Shaw since their inception. They sent her a demo tape and a lengthy letter. Judging the tape to be 'noisy rubbish', Shaw sent it back. They sent her another tape. Shaw sent that one back too. (It's fair to point out that she had grown suspicious of modern collaborations after her previous disastrous involvement with the BEF 'Music Of Quality And Distinction' version of 'Anyone Who Had A Heart'.)

Undaunted, Marr and Morrissey went to see Shaw at her home and plied her with spiel. She formed an immediate trust and liking for the duo, and it was on the basis of that trust that she agreed to record with them. She still, at this point, disliked the songs and it wasn't until she was in the studio and involved that she found a passionate core to the music and began to revel in it. Something began to dawn on Sandie Shaw. Although she had consistently turned away from singing opportunities – "The more people nagged, the more I was determined to stay away" – she realised that this was something that, say, Lulu would never even consider. (Lulu's equivalent would probably be her working of David Bowie's 'Man Who Sold The World', an altogether more lightweight idea despite the genius of the song). Originally,

the Sandie Shaw A-side was going to be 'I Don't Owe You Anything' but the revived freshness of 'Hand In Glove' virtually powered its way on to the A-side.

Released amid a wave of publicity, Shaw's 'Hand In Glove' reached number 27 and resulted in one bizarre Top Of The Pops appearance. One envisages mums and dads throughout the country saying, "Ooh good, Sandie Shaw is back. Better than this modern rubbish," only to be confronted by a leather clad Sandie, writhing about the Top Of The Pops floor with an equally leather clad Smiths behind her engaged in a bitter battle over individual volume.

"THE SUN SHINES OUT OF OUR BEHINDS..".

Sandie's vocals, clear as crystal, slipped joyfully into her Morrissey role. It seemed as if she'd been awaiting this opportunity for years. The celebratory burial of the shoeless waif. It looked, for all the world, as if she really didn't give a damn.

She guested on 'Hand In Glove' at the climax to The Smiths show at The Hammersmith Palais. Before her appearance she sat by the edge of the stage completely terrified. As the band left the stage (she appeared only for the encore) they couldn't find her and panicked, thinking that she'd hated the show and gone home. In the nick of time they discovered her in a state of hapless stage fright. Later, at three in the morning, after the post show chaos and ligging had succumbed to weariness, Morrissey rang her and said, "Well?".

She told him that she could have stayed onstage for hours, that it had been the most exhilarating experience of her life. To this day, this remains Morrissey's proudest moment.

It seemed that Sandie Shaw's emotive handling of the task was fired by an intense and intelligent hatred towards the attitudes of performers involved in modern pop music. Speaking to *Record Mirror's* Graham K, she emitted all the maturity of a media mother figure: "I hate that desperation people have. It's always been much better if you're more natural. If you are doing something which *feels* right. That's why I stopped before. It wasn't fun...I don't particularly enjoy being famous. I can't understand why people want to be pop stars. The thought of that album and tour routine – it's so boring...I can't believe the single mindedness which the new girls work at getting themselves across. My ambitions are much broader and more personal. Music isn't my life any more." And Morrissey? "Well, if he works a bit harder he might come on...I'd like to see him have a few failures and see how he handles that."

This is a little odd considering The Smiths' make up, was up to this point, completely based on experience of

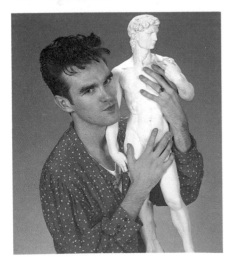

failure. What the world really wanted to know was how The Smiths would handle lasting success? Intentional or not, it was the Sandie Shaw episode which first brought the Smiths' sense of style into focus. Morrissey, in *Record Mirror*, modelled a black linen suit to complement Sandie Shaw's black halter neck dress. It was obviously a send-up of *The Face* but it nevertheless reflected a certain smartening up in the band. Not renowned for sartorial elegance, The Smiths had previously used their ill fitting and faded attire to maintain the connection with their low tech background. With outstanding success behind them, they used their eccentricities of taste (and newly acquired cash) to move a little upmarket.

They saw it as a move away from a possible patronising stance of deliberate scruffdom. Unlike their Mancunian rivals New Order, they were willing to prove that a sense of style wasn't necessarily a barometer of blandness. They would never be Spandau Ballet. They did look a little absurd though, with Morrissey's quiff looming in enormous proportions and Marr's face speedily reclining behind a blossoming mop of fringe. Caricature was just around the corner. The press photos for Sandie's 'Hand In Glove' showed The Smiths, for the first time, looking like a pop band. A Morrissey interview nestled comfortably within the pages of *The Face*.

Johnny Marr: "I steal most of my ideas for style directly from the Perry boys of Salford. They are incredibly stylish people. The best dressed youth in the world, the most sussed. They are so far ahead of London it's not true."

Rourke and Joyce dutifully pressed seams into their Levi's. Morrissey printed his new found image on to postcards and sent them to all his friends and closest followers. And a few enemies.

SIX.

FANS

"I was happy in the haze
of the drunken hour,
But heaven knows
I'm miserable now".

(from 'Heaven Knows…')

The hymn-like 'Heaven Knows I'm Miserable Now' was a testament to the fact that success didn't automatically breed contentment…but it helps.

Hardly a title to conjure up visions of wild youthful abandonment, 'Heaven Knows…' pushed The Smiths further into the badlands of bedsit squalor, a Godsend for those who couldn't stomach the effortless polish of Sade. The Smiths lay on top of Everything But The Girl and, as the hearts of the trenchcoat hordes re-opened, the flak from disgruntled outsiders intensified once more. 'Heaven Knows I'm Miserable Now' was a hymn of drunken melancholy; reflective, beyond bitterness, remote, superficially negative and sincere. 'Heaven Knows…' conjured up all the possible visions of hopelessness. Stuck firmly in the 'What's the point' vein, the song contained a dangerous element of the suicidal. Morrissey was attempting to come to terms with the emptiness of success which, in moments of depression, was as numbing as past days of failure. It was certainly the band's strongest single to date and yet, in the commercial world, their weakest onslaught.

The use of the word 'miserable' was a deliberate provocation of the obvious and did little but invite criticism. The record seemed to openly encourage the backlash which, amazingly, The Smiths had thus far avoided. But a press backlash did kick into gear, leaving a handful of diehard music writers to fight a bitter battle.

Reviewing the song in *Record Mirror*, Dylan Jones wrote: "The predictable and unnecessary Smiths backlash is now in full flight but can anyone dislike such a masterful song as this? The branch-adorned Morrissey sings his maudlin way through the personal lament of the week – a soaring ballad that deserves lots of attention so don't get caught in the bushfire, backlashers."

Interesting to note that in a week where Madonna, Nick Heyward, Tracie, The Pretenders and Siouxsie and The Banshees all released singles, only the low key meanderings of The Smiths were to find fruition as hit material. Pop music (as in chart music) has a habit of sweeping whole areas aside to make way for newer, equally lightweight material from an equally sickly new wave. That this had no effect on The Smiths was a sign of the lasting nature of their true audience. They were tagged 'miserable sods' – a label that soon became a standing joke – and the arguments raged. The Smiths became the over-used reference point in many a puerile pub argument . . .

 miths fan Dave Haslam, Stockport: "The thing is that The Smiths are the only human band in England. Even the people I've followed like U2, Echo & The Bunnymen and New Order are just pale by comparison. I understand what Morrissey is saying because he lives his life like me."

New Order fan Paul Clayton, Bury: "Morrissey is no different than any other pop star. I think The Smiths have made some good music but all this humanity stuff is just patronising and utterly dishonest. At least New Order don't pretend to be anything other than musicians which is an honest statement for once. They don't pretend to offer us anything so they can't let us down. Morrissey has just become a star so all this 'I'm a misery' shit, will not reflect his lifestyle. How can it? He is up there and having a great time. Nothing wrong with that. He deserves it as much as anyone, maybe more, but I just wish he wouldn't be so patronising."

It may be a case for argument that people are less willing to accept patronising notions from people in superior positions. (I couldn't get Tony Benn to comment on that one so we'll have to make do with Radio One's Janice Long). "Not patronising in the least. Intelligent music lovers require more than a pout from Simon Le Bon or a wiggle or is it a riddle from Nik Kershaw. The Smiths are a no fuss, no frills band who have taken music a step forward. That's got to be a good thing."

On the other hand, a wiggle or a riddle from Nik Kershaw surely doesn't hold any aspirations other than being unpretentious entertainment. There is certainly a case for both approaches. The Smiths, though, have little time for the live and let live view.

Speaking in *Record Mirror* , Johnny Marr answered accusations of arrogance accordingly: "It always surprises me that people should call us arrogant or pretentious. When we first started we were sick of the way many groups would adopt a cool persona for interviews. Our interviews were always embarrassingly honest and unpremeditated...The Thompson Twins, Howard Jones, Nik Kershaw are the epitome of what is wrong with the record buying public. Everyone has got so used to safe, tidy music. When 'This Charming Man' was unleashed on the general public it did sound really fresh and exciting."

But such are the mutterings of the oldest argument in the rock book. Only those who buy records hold the key to success.

hris Young, Chelmsford: "If you were to believe that people buy a record by The Smiths because they wish to change something, even if it is only the music industry, then I think you are

43

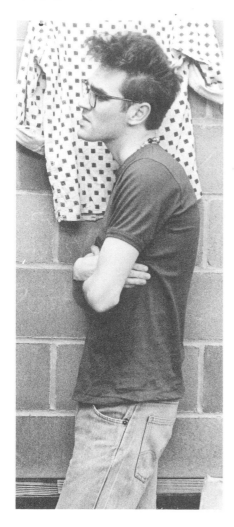

being very naïve about things. Surely everyone learnt lessons
when bands like The Clash let everyone down. When a band
stops making good records then people stop buying them.
I've bought Smiths records but they have never altered my
way of thinking. I think Morrissey sees himself as some sort
of father figure and I think that is why he gets people's backs
up."

Heroes always let you down. As Tony Parsons
and Julie Burchill once stated: "It's only rock and roll and it's
plastic, plastic, yes it is."

Back in The Haçienda, tweed trousered, shorn
haired, Mark Radcliffe had different views: "The music you
listen to is like the way you dress, the films you like or the
books you read, a statement about yourself. If you like bland
pieces of art then you'll probably be a bland person. It is
almost a proof that you are not willing to think about things.
I'm not saying that trendy clothes make a better person,
possibly the reverse is true, but it's the whole spectrum of
youth culture. Like when someone says that the records you
love are just plastic junk and they are the sort of people who
read and take in all that shit in the daily papers, then it makes
me think that my daily intake of media is far superior to
theirs. The Smiths, yeah, they are a thinking man's band.
They are more than just a money machine. It's obvious that
Morrissey has a lot to say and if people weren't ready to listen
then they wouldn't be so successful. They played in here and
slagged the place off which I thought was a bit pathetic but I
don't pretend to like all their ideas. I mean, I don't swallow
everything Morrissey says but I'll always consider him worth
listening to."

The legendary Jon the Postman, (the ultimate fan
of seventies punk who achieved minor fame by clambering
on to the stage and reciting 'Louie Louie' at the finish of
every Buzzcocks gig): "The Smiths are a great rock'n'roll
band. Simple as that. You can get drunk and dance to them
or you can listen intently to the lyrics. I live in San Francisco
now and The Smiths have a massive underground following
over there. There is a new wave of guitar bands springing up
over there, it's really exciting, just like British punk and, you
know, The Smiths are the only British band which fans of this
movement will accept."

Tony Wilson: "No comment."

Piccadilly Radio D.J. Tony Michaelides: "It's
just down to the fact that they make extremely good records.
They are successful because of that, above all else."

Mark E. Smith: "No comment".

Mancunian freelance music writer Ro Newton:
"The fans of The Smiths seem to be in the foreground before
the band themselves. The Interflora boom and Smiths
devotees were sprouting up all over the place with their
obnoxious shirts and silly haircuts. Perhaps it was the
Mancunian manic depressive bliss that was so alluring.

Morrissey is the martyr – confessing to almost every social stigma in the book and finding pleasure in pain. From the first album on The Smiths matured from semi-suicidal to sensitive, with their much needed plausible pop-marketable yet meaningful approach, which is rare enough these days. The most appealing aspect of The Smiths is their charisma – working class street boys make good but still retain an aura of mystery. The Smiths have never really conformed to the pop ideal, being larger than life but twice as monotonous, although some would disagree. They have a cult status which remains something of an enigma – particularly in the North-west where they stand for all that is dreary and depressing.

"*Coronation Street* and The Smiths go hand in hand in the same way that you could couple Frankie with *Brookside* – two necessary focal points of each city, at least for those south of the ship canal and the Mersey. The Smiths have given Manchester something to be proud of – an identity which, in itself, is not all that healthy.

"The city is too easily stereotyped as a bleak and industrial wasteland full of flat-capped frustrated poets and musos consoling themselves with endless amounts of ale. But what, for instance, does Morrissey know about life, sat in his living room in Halebarns denouncing carnivores everywhere when some poor bugger in Hulme would give his right arm for a pork chop?

"Just how long can he continue to draw on the northern W.C. subculture to fuel his quill or equally abused topics of consternation? There will come a time when that joke isn't funny any more. Until then, The Smiths appear to have the upper hand."

Ex-*Sounds* writer Dave McCullouch: "I think The Smiths have moved so far away from their original ideals. For one thing they are impossible to reach now and that isn't the way it has to be, it's just the way it always is. The Smiths have this superstar aura about them now which is certainly not what I thought they would grow into. I just can't fathom what they are about any more."

Easterhouse guitarist Ivor: "Well, we knew The Smiths from years ago. We used to be their pet band until we had a rather silly disagreement onstage. I mean, they were very good to us so I'm not complaining. They are still one of the few bands who mean anything these days. The disagreement? Oh well, it was nothing really. Johnny Marr was acting like a superstar on stage and the gig finished with Andy, our singer, threatening to hit him. I think they went off us after that although I'm still friendly with Morrissey".

Obviously The Smiths make a fine point of conversation which, in itself, is proof that they touch people with various degrees of impact. Just that they are worthy of debate, is, itself, an unusual compliment.

This didn't stop the rock press from gnashing its teeth and a prize was certainly in the offing for the writer who

could effectively belittle the Morrissey figure. However, apart from a continuous and fairly boring trickle of snide remarks in the gossip columns (mainly digs at Morrissey's claims to a celibate lifestyle), nothing of any real harm was seen in print.

Dave McCullouch: "I remember once, though, when *Sounds* were searching for an interview and I happened to know that the whole thing was a set-up. I knew it was a deliberate attempt from the word go to bring the band down. I rang the band's manager and told him so. The interview was cancelled."

As Morrissey settled into a London-based summer, Johnny Marr dabbled with outside projects. He spent time in Strawberry Studios in Stockport laying down a guitar part for Factory based Quando Quango, a surprising move on two accounts. Firstly, Quando Quango's roots were firmly planted within disco electrofunk. Quando remained a little known cult band in England but aspired to a high degree of success in the New York dance floor market. Little more than a rhythm section revolving around a Lynn Drum, they were Factory's fairly successful attempt at New York chicness, and Factory desperately wanted to become an important international concern. Although the style of Quando was totally alien to Marr, he enjoyed the challenge immensely and his quickly learnt funk guitar added a spark of humanity to the proceedings. The union of Marr and Quando was also seen as a peace treaty between The Smiths and The Factory organisation. Quando's lead singer and saxophonist, Mike Pickering, was also the official booker for bands at The Haçienda.

Marr thoroughly enjoyed his status as Manchester's ambassador for modern music. He bought a white 1964 Rover 2.6 Litre and spent much time speeding between Morrissey's Kensington pad and Manchester. Joyce and Rourke spent their days looking noticeable within the boozy confines of The Haçienda. Meanwhile Morrissey made a brief appearance between the pages of *No. 1* when the magazine had the interesting idea of flying Morrissey to Liverpool for a tape recorded chat with Echo & The Bunnymen's outspoken Ian McCullouch. The idea was to test the conflict between the bitter-swilling working class intellect of Mac and the supposedly more refined nut-chewing idealism of Morrissey. It was one of the few times that the pulp glossy pop press produced journalism worth reading. Both Mac and Morrissey were well known for slagging off the entire rock world outside their small circles. Would they turn on each other? Well, no, but an interesting verbal tennis match did take place.

Morrissey: "A lot of groups from Manchester are more intelligent than groups from other places."

Mac: "No, I think they are more studious…as in having copies of 'De Profundis' under their arms. In Liverpool it is a lot harder for people to accept that a poet is possibly what you are…"

Morrissey: "People in Liverpool have more humour. Everything is hilarious. There is something naïve about the city which is treasurable. Manchester·is more ugly. In Liverpool things have been restored whereas in Manchester they just crush the past without a second thought. That reflects on the people."

Mac: "The difference between Manchester and Liverpool groups is that Liverpool has never had a university tradition."

Morrissey: "A joint concert? I'd love to do it."

Mac: "It might even be important in some way. I thought it might be like a clan gathering…but why the hell should it be. If certain people don't congregate, it becomes friction."

Morrissey: "Or segregation."

Mac: "When it doesn't need to be. If I sounded dubious about The Smiths, it's because they represented the first threat to us."

Morrissey: "I think that the best groups can co-exist. I feel rivalry and anger at most groups but the cream of what this country has can co-exist quite amicably together."

Mac: "I mean he'll keep saying The Smiths are the best and I'll…"

Which is back-slapping of the highest order. The pair basked in a shared arrogance; arrogance not aimed at the kid in the street but arrogance aimed at Britain's pop aristocracy. Both The Smiths and Echo & The Bunnymen offer a complete dismissal of Camden Palace élitism. Manchester/Liverpool rivalry aside, the meeting was important because it took place in a magazine which is a vehicle for the Spandaus, Durans and Marilyns of this world to say "Hey look at me. I'm in rock and roll. Aren't I fucking great". By simply existing in a successful role, both bands are effectively working against that mentality.

Sade hates The Smiths. The Smiths hate Sade. Morrissey hates synthesizers. Neither Morrissey nor Mac would later be asked to take part in the Band Aid single and neither gave a damn.

As willing outcasts from British pop society, The Smiths were holding true to their original promise; that, despite the stories of their inflating egos, they were remaining on course…and beautifully aloof. From the quotes on previous pages, only one stood out as surprising. As one who was so instrumental in mapping out the future promise of early Smiths, his quote "If you asked me to write

something about The Smiths now it would probably be critical'', remained interesting. I thought it would be interesting to ask him to do just that and hereby present…

THE DAVE McCULLOUCH MINI CHAPTER: "Reflections on The Smiths, a pop band. I think I did say, in print, in *Sounds*, that they would be the last major rock band, in the sense that they would follow, and terminate, the trend that rolls through The Who/The Stones etc, playing big stadiums on summer days to hordes of worshippers.

"In hindsight, that mightn't have been far wrong. The Smiths as far as I was concerned were obviously going to be massive, *what-they-now-are*. That four square classic line up. And Morrissey.

"Also, the timing. Very important. Every now and then the timing is *just right* for that four square magic to be stirred again. Hence, Smithmania.

"I think it's gone wrong somewhere. Maybe I was hoping for the impossible – that they'd control their situation once they reached the football stadiums. Treat it with dashes of irony, danger, threat…use contrasts. What we have is them *merely* following awful Bunnymen in playing the ridiculous Albert Hall. Grammar school rock may give Morrissey the perfect adoring audience for his ramblings but it does not help the wider case of rock or rock's present stagnancy. This is selfish of him in the true sense.

"They release too many records into an already over-crowded scene. Not much literary grace there, Steven. This lacks dignity and is almost certainly due to Morrissey's long years of neglect. Now he's in the limelight we'll have everything he can throw at us – hardly a recipe for the group's long standing. I fear, I strongly suspect, that this is the route to blowing yourself away. Like football, rock careers need pacing. He never seems to look outside the context of his group. He'll sponsor James but that only serves to make James-Smiths clones. Every time The Smiths play a traditional fifty dater around the country they kill off five budding James by buttressing the more dangerous music biz clichés. All of this isn't controlling your situation. It is in fact showing the discerning outside eye that The Smiths are, proverbially in rockspeak, well messed up.

Key words in the rise of The Smiths:

LUCK: They wept at me virtually that they were told by Rough Trade, that they were a "minor Rough Trade" group. Without boasting, this led to ME going OTT in *Sounds* in an attempt, that was successful, to change that. That saved Rough Trade's bacon, as it turned out.

FAITH: The enormous faith of their audience, matching that of U2's audience and, earlier, that which Paul Weller used to trade on. It reveals the desperation of kids to get something from rock. That Morrissey isn't giving anything real other than stock Man Of The People. A wag schtick grieves me. He should have more critics.

APOGEE: Smiths were an apogee in the sense that everything on the scene turned on and with them, like a fulcrum.

      The Smiths could be said to have done a final demolition job on punk rock '76 style. They have reinforced, unwittingly, all the pre-punk music biz values. To me they are a sad sight. To see a *threat-that-was* coming across as anything but a threat is saddening. They have a music biz ring through their noses: the last rock band. Surely they will provide the final lesson that rock 'n' roll needs more thinking, more philosophising in a real sense before we can ever allow another four-square Smiths to appear, vastly entertaining but also clutching their own downfall.

That The Smiths are the most popular group, in rough terms, at the precise time that rock 'n' roll is going through its worst phase for many years says something that is not complimentary to them. Which is saying: Smiths are the victim of the vast cliché-ing in rock, whereby everything is not as it seems, i.e. note the present glut of supposed 'leftish' groups signing to major labels: Billy Bragg as the opposite of Wham. 'He's good, they're not' etc.

Ironically, Morrissey being a great thinker, The Smiths dilemma shows that just not enough thought is put into rock. What it is for? What is it about? What state is it in? Where is it going to? Who does it affect and how does it affect them?

As Morley and ZTT hint, we haven't even *begun* to kick around this thing called rock. Smiths are, unfortunately, helping to bolster up all those cruds still clinging to the starting line and holding the starting gun. They are the last rock 'n' roll band before a new and better rock 'n' roll race/creed begins. In history they will be seen as trapped, important and the most sensational and magnificent rock 'n' roll failure ever. And I really do dread Morrissey's solo career, once they have split. I bet he shaves his head and turns Hindu.

While not agreeing with all of the above, McCullouch's sentiments have an unnerving knack of echoing 'exactly' the underlying theme of this book (as mentioned in the foreword) without prior discourse between myself and McCullouch. Where The Smiths escape condemnation here is that, although The Smiths are certainly Super-glued to rock's traditional methods, they are using those methods to push across more important sentiments stemming from way deeper than the plastic and unimportant workings of the music business. I'm not so romantic to be able to place too much importance in this area. I suspect, though, that Morrissey is. However, if his quest was originally to break down the stranglehold of the rock system, would he have settled for such a four square traditional format? The Smiths fit boringly into the tour and album syndrome. Their Mancunian counterparts, New Order, don't. They prefer to play spasmodic gigs in unconventional places, but in the end…what difference does it make?

It makes none because whereas The Smiths attract the same kind of audience (who hold intense faith) as U2 and The Jam (which is basically the male dominated sexually repressed types who are also the essence of heavy metal) they still refuse to display the schoolboy phoney surreal imagery of those people. There is a more humble and positive value attached to Morrissey's lyricism. But…do The Smiths move the mind or do The Smiths move the body? I don't know.

And then came the second Fleet Street sensation.

seven

"William, it was really nothing".

As The Thompson Twins solidified their position as 'the band Simon Bates likes to name drop most often', as Bronksi Beat (despite their obvious sincerity) continually resembled a whistling kettle, and as Depeche Mode turned sado/masochism into such a lightweight subject that it wouldn't cause offence if your four year old daughter played 'Master And Servant', The Smiths were to be heard crooning the very odd 'William, It Was Really Nothing': "And everybody's got to live their life and God knows I've got to live mine".

Such liberalism seemed to fit into any climate, any mass of chart pulp, even a chart filled by girls in silly hats.

There was Morrissey, again on Top Of The Pops, again without a video. There was Morrissey crooning away. The nation looked on and failed to notice the difference. So there was a singer with a funny shirt on. So what? Those who looked hard enough could easily appreciate the difference between the Twins pouting and swaying to 'Doctor Doctor' and The Smiths by now legendary pastiche performances, but to the average Top Of The Pops viewer and the average record buyer, the difference was non existent.

'William, It Was Really Nothing' had a backbone made of a far more substantial nature. Topped with the typical cynical yet liberal chorus, 'William It Was Really Nothing' appeared as a complete condemnation of the 'Glenda Brownlow' approach towards marriage; simply another of Morrissey's attempts to dispense with a traditionally Northern, working class system, an assault on an institution which effectively freezes two people into whatever mundane existence they live, as a blindly accepted method of halting all ambition. Of course marriage can have the opposite effect but this is largely the virtue of a middle class pact. It could be, and often is, a successful method of keeping the working class in their place.

Morrissey's self promoted celibacy ran directly against this particular macho gain. Naïve as it may sound, Morrissey's ideals (which ran opposite to the "If he doesn't get himself a missis soon he'll be left on the shelf…or he's a pooftah.." mentality) attracted many admirers. Part of the essence of rock 'n' roll is a young person's thoughtful dismantling of archaic virtues, a completely natural function and yet, superficially, a blindly rebellious one. Nobody likes to see their mistakes exposed in public, especially those who have to spend the rest of their lives in bitter consequence.

Surprisingly, the opposition to 'William It Was Really Nothing' came not from an older generation (who, obviously weren't even aware of the record) but from the feminist movement long since supported and admired by Morrissey. They saw it as an attack on feminine intelligence. It so obviously wasn't and the argument is, by now, nothing but heresay.

The second Fleet Street sensation was no laughing matter. The offence, which was always delicately balanced, was caused by 'Suffer Little Children'. The song made a re-appearance as the flip side to 'Heaven Knows I'm Miserable Now' and was brought to the attention of relatives of the murdered 'Moors' children – Lesley Ann Downey and John Kilbride. One relative, understandably upset, rang *The Manchester Evening News* who used the outrage as a lead story, giving The Smiths the kind of publicity no band would relish. (Feelings in Manchester, especially in the Hyde area, had always run high in regard to the moors murders. The area would never forget and equally wouldn't take kindly to some pop group dabbling in the tragedy).

The resulting chaos saw the Boots and Woolworths chains withdrawing both the album and single from their shops.

Boots: "We had a complaint from the Kilbride family and as a result of that we withdrew both album and single, as there were words which tended to be offensive to the family."

Woolworths: "The Manchester Evening News telephoned us to say that one of the relatives had complained that we were selling records by this band The Smiths. We played the song and had a discussion. There was an investigation and we decided to take the records off sale altogether."

To the general public, it looked like a particularly cheap and horrendous way of gaining publicity. The spokesman from Rough Trade took great care before releasing the following statement: "The Smiths stand 100% behind the lyrics to all their songs. 'Suffer Little Children' is no exception. The song was written out of profound emotion by Morrissey, a Mancunian who feels that the particularly horrific crime it describes must be borne by the conscience of Manchester and that it must never happen again. It was written out of deep respect for the victims and their kin, and The Smiths felt it was an important enough song to put on their last single even though it had already been released on their L.P. In a word it is a memorial to the children and all like them who have suffered such a fate. The Smiths are acknowledged as writing with sensitivity, depth and intelligence and the suggestion that they are cashing in on a tragedy at the expense of causing grief to the relatives of its victims is absolutely untrue.

"Morrissey has had a lengthy conversation with the mother of Lesley Ann Downey, Mrs West, and she understands that the intentions of the song are completely honourable. Furthermore, he is willing to speak to any immediate members of the families involved so there will be no misunderstanding."

There was, as it happened, one more chilling coincidence. On the cover of the 'Heaven Knows...' was an old photograph of Viv Nicholson which was used to portray the sentiments of the A-side. But the photograph resembled Myra Hindley and was taken as such in many quarters, especially by the scandal hungry tabloids who were fast turning The Smiths into some kind of sinister platform for the beliefs of the wicked Morrissey. Morrissey, still the object of scorn for his apparently traitorous move to London, was considering a move back to the plush surrounds of Hale Barns (home of many a former Manchester City player) in Cheshire. His reasons had much to do with the continuous hounding by London journalists.

Morrissey was deeply upset by the 'Suffer Little Children' episode, but he shouldn't have been surprised. Although it is beyond doubt that the group's motives were strictly honourable, they were always fully aware of the intensely emotive nature of the subject. They knew, from day one, the possibility of causing offence and that their case would be misconstrued in the media. If a mistake was made, it was lifting 'Suffer Little Children' on to the back of the single, a decision which was entirely down to the band. But The Smiths now found that success tends to complicate situations which made their initial stance of well meant integrity and the desire to do things differently ("We don't wish to become pop stars") a virtual impossibility.

Take, for instance, the subject of touring. As a group develops, it slowly attains a responsibility towards the people who work for it. Suddenly there is a regular road crew who become attached to the band. The crew have families and need work, and as they become virtual employees of the band, the band has to act with appropriate responsibility. This works to 'dull' a band's sense of adventure and as the work rate intensifies, it is a natural reaction to concentrate on artistic input and leave the fundamentals (tour organisation and administrative chores) to those employed for the purpose.

A rumour began to circulate around the cocktail bars of the music biz élite that The Smiths were unhappy with Rough Trade and, although still tied with contracts, were seeking to move away. Obviously every record company in Britain wasted no time in sniffing out the possibilities of picking up the band. (A band of this stature would be worth a costly legal battle). Equally obviously, Rough Trade were determined to quell these rumours.

Strangely enough, it was Factory Records who were reported to be the front runners, but these rumours were strongly denied by Factory.

All this resulted in an angry Geoff Travis (founding supremo of Rough Trade) saying: "If anyone wants The Smiths they'll have to give Rough Trade three million and me personally another three million." This deliberately throwaway remark hints at the paranoia within the ranks of Rough Trade where The Smiths are the only band of stature that they had managed to retain. (In the past, Rough Trade acts who achieved major success like say, Aztec Camera, walked into the more solid foundations of a major company). However, as the wheels within wheels of the music industry continue to grind, the question of exactly what *is* an independent company comes into focus.

The Smiths, for example, while signed to Rough Trade, are handled and distributed by the major London Records. A minor band signed to London like, say, Easterhouse, are fully distributed by Rough Trade. So exactly who is the independent band? We are told it's The Smiths who remain qualified to compete in the independent charts despite whatever gigantic deals may take place in the background. This mess of confusion is a direct result of the majors' steadily regaining the control which was threatened by the rise of the independent labels in the late seventies. The suggestion that The Smiths represent a threat to the gigantic conglomerates who control the basic music industry is false. Even Rough Trade itself, as with all other successful indies, has been effectively integrated into the fabric of the bulk industry. What The Smiths have gained, by remaining with Rough Trade, has been a far greater artistic control. Morrissey has been able to design all the record covers and, with the possible exception of 'This Charming Man New York', the band have remained as decision makers in regard to single releases, a measure of control practically unheard of in larger companies.

To all other intents and purposes then, The Smiths are a major band with major backing.

eight

HATFUL OF HOLLOW
"I would love to go back
to the old house...
But I never will...
I never will".
(from 'Back To The Old House')

As the eventful summer of 1984 faded into autumn, The Smiths eased into a deliberate fade from media attention. They kept a low profile in Liverpool's Amazon Studio, rehearsing and working on new material. Taken somewhat aback by the speed and scope of their success, and worried about the proverbial 'bursting bubble', they planned no future releases until well into the new year.

There are two schools of thought about the early November release of 'Hatful of Hollow'. One is that Rough Trade panicked. Fast approaching was the immensely lucrative Christmas market, and their biggest selling act had no plans nor any desire to throw product into the mad spending spree. Hence, the speedy release of the 'false album', 'Hatful of Hollow'. Nobody could be blamed for thinking the worst. Releasing a collection of radio sessions with a few previously unavailable songs in perfect timing for

Christmas *does* appear to be begging for critical crucifixion. However, due to the unusual position the band found themselves in, I prefer to believe the second official theory. A huge amount of mail poured into Rough Trade's offices demanding some form of release of the legendary Smiths radio sessions. This demand from fans also highlights the fact that those sessions contained a far more lively and adventurous sound than on the dowdy first album.

Morrissey: "As far as we are concerned those are the sessions which got us excited in the first place and apparently it was how a lot of people discovered us also."

Indeed, the freshness and simplicity of those recordings played a vital part in laying the foundations of a lasting career. It was those sessions which won the band initial recognition and a recording contract. It seemed a perfect opportunity to satisfy the twin hungers of record company and fans alike. For the band it was an effortless release, effectively supplying a breathing space…and lastly, making more money.

Despite the odd slap in the *NME,* 'Hatful Of Hollow' received scant criticism and deservedly so. The songs, pulled directly from the John Peel and Dave Jensen sessions, were added to the last two singles and B-sides and scattered, with perfect pacing, across a 16-track LP which was to retail at no more than £3.99 (providing the retailers kept the faith which, largely, they did). Not only was this excellent value but it provided, for the first time, the full breadth and vision of The Smiths on album format. Whereas 'The Smiths' struggled, but failed, to climb out of a one dimensional musical format, 'Hatful Of Hollow' contained a wide variety of styles and experiments coloured by the straightforward production and flavoured by the clearly audible voice of Morrissey. The most precious moments were the Marr-ed acoustic marriages of guitar and reverb-drenched vocals on 'Back To The Old House' and

'Please, Please, Please, Let Me Get What I Want'. Both songs sandwiched 'Reel Around The Fountain' at the close of side two and effectively allowed the album to slide quietly away in a dreamily emotive condition.

Facts: 'Hatful Of Hollow' was a complete accident. 'Hatful Of Hollow' was The Smiths finest piece of plastic to date. 'Hatful Of Hollow' was to spend a happy Christmas in the top five of the album chart. And it had other things going for it too.

As the bulk of the material was culled from just three radio sessions, this proved that an album of quality could still be made for less than the cost of recording your average chart single. Technological advances within the recording industry, although providing interesting new extensions on popular noise, have had a number of diverse effects. The scramble for perfect vinyl ambience has forced record companies into sending their spotty new acts into the most highly sophisticated 'digital' recording studios in the country. A producer is chosen to mould the natural sound of the band into the new format, and the mesmerised band wander out of the studio clutching a product bearing little or no resemblance to the demo they went in with. As the battle for success is so brutal, the band rarely complain. This accepted method of producing conveyor belt muzak also creates a huge gulf between the music of signed acts and that of unsigned acts or bands on smaller independent labels. As public taste develops an acceptance of such modern noise, public taste turns away from low tech, cheaply made musics; one more factor in chipping away the importance of talent. The most successful group in Britain at this time was Frankie Goes To Hollywood whose career was manufactured for them. In the beginning all the band had was one hook line. More importantly, in the beginning all the band *needed* was one hook line. People were awed by the 'sound' of Frankie. The song remained alarmingly unimportant.

'Hatful Of Hollow', despite the carefully scrubbed edges, came complete with a 'sound' well within the reach of any band...well, almost. The simplistic edges succeeded in highlighting the strength of the songwriting, the virtuosity of Johnny Marr's guitar work and the gradual coming together of four musicans with one purpose. These were all traditional 'naked' plus factors, all perpetrating a certain purity and old fashioned virtue. And yet, there was 'Hatful Of Hollow' doing business with the ultra smooth plastic perfection of Sade, the pop bubble and squeak of Wham and the mega-hype of Frankie Goes To Hollywood. Yet again, The Smiths headed the forefront of the backlash. Beautifully out of time, they proved that all the paranoia which surrounds those seeking to hitch a ride on the next bandwagon is worthless. The Smiths succeeded because they followed their natural instincts and disregarded the trendiness of the moment. 'Hatful Of Hollow' remains as a

testament to that fact. (Common sense really, the music business works in a very slow yet haphazard fashion. To copy currently successful trends is to place yourself two years behind… instantly).

Many bands saw 'Hatful Of Hollow' as a measure of possibilities within their grasp. Nobody but a fool who believes that luck lies around the corner could be similarly influenced by the likes of Frankie.

Despite the criticism of a false Christmas onslaught, 'Hatful Of Hollow' was a beautifully typical indication of The Smiths general attitude. The lack of expense involved complies fully with their famous refusal to produce promo videos. As the music business increasingly places so much importance on the look (A & R men no longer listen to the music first: the priority of the A & R man is to envisage how the band will look on video) so The Smiths abhor such methods. They strongly believe that enough image is apparent from the lyrics and is fully complemented by the (often Morrissey designed) sleeve imagery.

Morrissey sees video as a dilution of lyrical emotion and a distraction from the lack of such within the song. If the all conquering trend towards video is to be challenged, then The Smiths will head that challenge. Putting it simply, it will only be beaten if public taste demands so. The true 'Godfather' of the music business is the public themselves. This said, The Smiths have little against the workings of a straight concert video.

Like every other band, The Smiths used to queue up at Factory, eagerly awaiting their videos off the Haçienda video production line. (One of the perks of playing the Haçienda was that the club offered a free video of a performance, something which turned sour as a massive backlog built up). Even so, the band have never felt at ease on film, even straight filming of concert performances. It is well reported that Johnny Marr's biggest regret is the filming of the BBC 2 *Sight And Sound* gig. Maybe, then, it is The Smiths' natural unease before cameras that has motivated their hatred of video. Whatever, the effect remains the same.

Fact: By relinquishing the responsibility of video, The Smiths retain the freedom to choose which singles are released. They also ease the pressure of financial commitment from the record company. As such, they are less sluggish than the average band.

The downside to this is that they lose valuable advertising space on television programmes such as *Saturday Superstore*. More importantly, they cannot compete in America on the, so far, massively successful cable broadcast *MTV*. This may be a fatal mistake. Just how they will fare when and if cable TV becomes a major selling vehicle in Britain is another poser for the future.

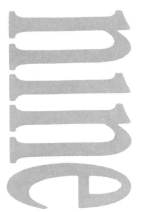

nine

"I decree today
that life is simply taking
and not giving.
England is mine,
It owes me a living".

(from 'Still Ill')

The four weeks preceding Christmas 1984 saw Britain locked in the desperate late stages of a long, cold and bitter conflict. The miners' strike failed to evolve into a veritable civil war (although, beneath the veneer of the tabloid media, it was getting pretty close) and a wave of pessimism was matched only by the resolve of the hardline few.

For better or worse, with sincerity or mercenary attachment, the hip musical climate was heavily involved. Political edge groups like The Redskins, Billy Bragg and The Three Johns held the music press to ransom, peddling their polemics while feverishly climbing their own ladders to success. (Nothing necessarily wrong with that). They spouted the need for hard line, no compromise, battle tactics and urged for the medium of rock/pop music to be used for propaganda purposes. Sensing a valuable communications network, the Kinnock-led Labour Party encouraged musical involvement. Everything pointed the way towards a better political awareness for young people. Well meant as it may have been, one wonders what accusations would have sprouted had the Tory Party used similar methods.

The apparent liberalism of Morrissey would seem to be a touch out of vogue here, although a hardening of his attitudes was clear during those few weeks. Without a record or any other reason to be in print, Morrissey was to be heard advocating the necessary use of political violence in support of CNDand in his approval of the Animal Liberation Front's great Mars Bar hoax. Morrissey now moved into outspoken areas, possibly as groundwork for the direction The Smiths were soon to follow.

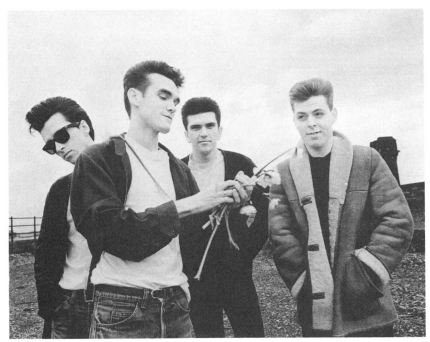

Bob Geldof, meanwhile, made a move of pure genius by inventing Band Aid. Geldof's idea and the money which was raised cannot be faulted, even if it was a pathetic sight to see the fat popsters fighting for the limelight. Morrissey was unimpressed. Later he would spit venom at Band Aid in an interview with *Time Out's* Simon Garfield.

"The whole implication was to save those people in Ethiopia, but who were they asking to save them? Some thirteen-year-old girl in Wigan. People like Thatcher and the Royals could solve the Ethiopian problem within ten seconds but Band Aid shied away from saying that. For heaven's sake, it was almost directly aimed at the unemployed."

Morrissey, though naturally a quiet and peaceful person, was never one to mince words. He caused many an offence during the Christmas period by openly stating his hatred of the Geldof coup. He opined that Band Aid was diabolical and that Geldof was a "nauseating character".

"In the first instance the record itself is absolutely tuneless", he said. "One can have a great concern for the people of Ethiopia, but it's another thing to inflict daily torture on the people of England. It is an awful record considering the mass of talent involved. And it wasn't done shyly, it was the most self righteous platform ever in the history of popular music."

Many felt sympathy with Morrissey's stance over this, but many didn't, preferring instead to follow Julie Burchill's line that Band Aid was the first record in the history of popular music that actually achieved a positive result; that Band Aid made the likes of The Redskins quake in their Doc Marten's and feel totally inconsequential.

It became clear that the shy, sensitive persona previously adopted by Morrissey was a thing of the past. Morrissey prepared to join the hardliners.

Such a call to arms was, in fact, a necessity for a band in their career situation. The thoughtful, sensitive emotions of both 'The Smiths' and 'Hatful Of Hollow' were the emotive products of impending poverty. The Smiths became special because those hardships were so obviously very real indeed. But no more. Suddenly inspiration had to come from an extremely private lifestyle, the classic Catch 22 of socialist rock and roll. Just as the scathing desperation of a band's early days helps fuel the sentiment and connect with an audience in a similar position, then a band's later lifestyle has no connection with the audience who, quite naturally, don't give a damn about the problems of being pop stars.

The Smiths would have to look outside. They would have to develop a wider vision.

Christmas in the music business brings a retrospective look at the best and worst moments of the preceding year. Nowhere is this more obvious than in the music press where critics collect their own charts, their own thoughts and their own egos. If nothing else, the Christmas editions of *NME, Sounds,* and *Melody Maker* are a barometer of hip opinion, although not so revealing as the readers' polls which follow a couple of months later.

The *NME* succumbed to The Smiths success by parading a lengthy Smiths interview by Biba Kopf, a writer not known for his enthusiasm for the Smiths. Although hardly succeeding in exposing the conflict between the band's artistic stance and their situation (which was the probable intention), the dual interview of Morrissey and Marr did, for once, produce worthy quotes.

Kopf: ''The Smiths are probably the oddest expression of that working class rage…Where do the Smiths stand in relation to those self appointed vents of working class spleen? Redskins? Seething Wells?''

Morrissey: ''Well, I don't want to be that extreme, though all the causes they stand behind I almost always agree with. I think audiences get bored with groups introducing strong hardcore politics into every song. You don't have to be madly blunt in a political sense. To me that lacks a certain degree of intellect and although we haven't made any abrasively bold political statements as such, I think people can gauge where we stand.''

Marr: ''…It isn't just nostalgia, it's northern spirit. A working man's spirit. I'm here trying not to sound like Gary Kemp doing the working class bit. But we are more about the working class values than we are about Rickenbackers and Brian Jones haircuts.''

Obviously…although Johnny Marr's two main obsessions in life do seem to be Rickenbackers and Brian Jones haircuts. But the above is representative of the general tone of the interview which constantly referred back to the suspiciously 'instant' political aspects of the band. They seemed determined to underline this, and use *NME* as a platform from which to begin the wind up towards the approaching 'Meat Is Murder' campaign.

Maybe it was an attempt to regain a certain 'hipness'. If it was, they needn't have bothered. Their audience extended way beyond anything threatened by the revolutionary dogma of the Redskins and for that matter the *NME*.

The writers' chart in the *NME* gave The Smiths a fair to low hearing, concentrating, as usual, on more obscure artifacts. In *Sounds*, the final round-up of the indie singles chart gave the band's number one and two with 'What Difference Does It Make' and 'Heaven Knows I'm Miserable Now' respectively with three other singles (if you count Sandie Shaw's little effort) in the top thirty. This was backed up by the famous John Peel's Festive Fifty which was embarrassingly dominated by the band. *Melody Maker* hid a definite nod of acceptance behind a peppering of harmless insults. The glossies followed suit, dutifully documenting the band's progress and blindly including this strange bunch of yokels among the smiling blonde beautiful masses. The Smiths were cast as eccentrics...which they are.

Morrissey, noted for his over-sensitive nature, wasn't taking the Christmas necessities very seriously. His forecast for 1985 in the *NME* led to nothing more than a throwaway: "Disability chic will reign rampantly in 1985. The hearing aid is replaced by the neck brace. No serious musicologist will be spotted in an audience minus a neck brace. Severe illness is rightly considered high art. Fab group of '85: James. Faded drama queen of '85: Midge Ure."

Which was nothing more than a sideways stab at *NME* hipness coupled with a nod towards the absurd fitness fad. Similar quotations were to be found in all the other Christmas and New Year music rags, all of which hinted at an unusually relaxed atmosphere within the band.

Work on the forthcoming album had practically been completed. (Cassettes of the album were already filtering into the higher regions of the music press). It had been a deliberate ploy to record the bulk of the tracks in Liverpool in order to keep The Smiths well and truly away from the metropolis of London. Morrissey was now settled in Hale Barns but, unlike the rest of the band, he was not seen in Manchester's trendier nightspots. His growing fear of public recognition is reflected in the story of a phone call to a leading Mancunian hairdresser's.

Female voice: "Can you send one of your stylists round. My client needs a hairdresser."

Receptionist: "I'm sorry, we don't work that way. Can't your client come to the salon".

Female voice: "Erm, Oh no. He couldn't possibly. Er…I mean…Oh dear. My client could never walk the streets of Manchester. It's…er…it's Morrissey."

A stylist was, in the end, dutifully sent on the mission but the situation was an alarming indication of Morrissey's inability to cope with the less enjoyable aspects of fame. In truth, with sensible precautions, Morrissey could have easily travelled to the salon.

Stories like this became commonplace in Manchester clubs where Morrissey gained a 'Pope of Pop' image that did little to maintain the stability of his early followers. Most such tales are unworthy of inclusion here and, in general, people tended not to believe them. But the 'no smoke without fire' theory remained in people's minds, all of which was a direct product of the band's status and a residue of success which leaves initial followers with a sense of loss as 'their' band goes public. Like Morrissey in 1977, many in Manchester felt left behind and even fairly close friends found it difficult to get close to the band. Taunts of 'Bloody Superstars' bear this out, but the sense of loss can be eased by deliberate attempts to spread bad rumour. This is, as Morrissey well knows, a perfectly natural human condition. A hyper-sensitive fellow, such things cause him great and needless upset but to the rest of the band, it is largely water off a duck's back, and they are dutifully protective of their singer, as are many of the people working around the band. Often this itself is misconstrued as a deliberate inaccessibility and leads to more 'superstar' taunts. (Throughout the production of this manuscript a wave of needless paranoia diluted my enquiries).

As 'Hatful Of Hollow' was a direct result of public demand, so the single from the album, 'How Soon Is Now', was a result of public request. First featured on the 12″ version of 'William, It Was Really Nothing', the song didn't reveal all its glory until heard within the context of 'Hatful'. Such was the reaction to the song that Rough Trade bravely released a single which already featured twice in the record collections of the die hard followers. The possibility of commercial suicide aside, the single was to become the perfect deflecting plate for the new album. It was also to become one of the biggest hits and the one provocative vinyl slap in a chart which reached new depths of blandness: Elaine Paige, King, Howard Jones, Foreigner and Russ Abbot. The haunting intensity of Johnny Marr's echoey guitar cut across a slow paced rhythm to create a sense of evil and Morrissey's line, "I am human and I need to be loved…just like everybody else does…", only succeeded in adding weight to the darkness.

Seeing Morrissey on Top Of The Pops mock machine gunning the audience added an element of comedy. (Wouldn't you like to machine gun the Top Of The Pops crowd?) There was a deeper side though, which reflected the singer's state of continual unhappiness. Forever boasting a totally celibate lifestyle, one sensed that Morrissey was confounded by his past lack of success with the opposite sex. He was once so alone that he needed to do something extraordinary in order to bring attention to himself. Those early days, when he shared a hovel with Linder and Ian Devine, were spent with few friends and 'How Soon Is Now', an indication that his personal situation hadn't improved with success, was hardly the typical Top Of The Pops sentiment of the day. Taking this verse into consideration brings an unmistakeable tinge of desperation of the "I am human…" line. Later in conversation with Nick Kent in The Face, Johnny Marr would admit: "Sometimes I think he is in need of a good humping."

'How Soon Is Now' is the ultimate example of Morrissey's insecurity and the feeling of abandonment which provided The Smiths with that vital fire. Their 'Why hasn't life improved then' sense of hopelessness points to Morrissey's overbearing terror, and, for him, it never can. On the other hand this is exactly the state of mind in which he loves to revel. His romantic notions of Oscar Wilde are fully acted out while he stays in this condition. It's not merely a false stance though: the only person who knows the real Morrissey, his mother, has proved this on many occasions by telephoning Rough Trade's office to complain about their handling of her delicate son.

The music paper reader polls which coincided with the success of 'How Soon Is Now' were the most important and final proof of the band's influence. Even so, the extent of their superiority was surprising. The magazine *Jamming* saw the band wipe the floor with all opposition in all categories outside the female sections. But, with respect to *Jamming* or *Melody Maker* the most influential readers' poll is undoubtedly in *NME*. The Smiths won best group, top songwriters, fourth and twelfth best LPs, three of the top twenty singles and Marr was top instrumentalist with Morrissey taking second best dressed person, fourth most wonderful human being and an appropriate placing in the 'creep of the year' award. All of which pushed The Smiths surprisingly above the more 'instant' Frankie Goes To Hollywood and implied that their following touched the size of The Jam's a few years previously. Rough Trade was already smacking its lips at the prospect of a massive selling LP.

Morrissey spent time writing 'thank yous' for all the music papers, lived in transit between Hale Barns and Kensington Hotels and prepared, with anxiety, for the prospect of a huge up and coming promotional tour. All hell was let loose as the pressure increased. Factory hopefuls James were constantly praised by The Smiths and, after a couple of successful shows in Ireland, secured the support spot for the tour. Sniffing greatness by association, in flocked the A & R men but with little luck as the bemused James turned their backs on record companies, turned down a chance to feature on the cover of *NME* (this was rectified later) and refused to supply photos in a strange but subtle disregard for the traditional career ladder. James would take the opportunity to tour, but couldn't sign simply as a by-product of The Smiths. Morrissey and Marr looked down like father figures.

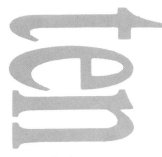

Meat Is Murder

It took just five days for 'Meat Is Murder' to give Rough Trade their first number one album. Therein lies a miracle of distribution. Someone, somewhere, within or around London Records managed to turn those frightening advance orders into material exchanges. Even the unbreakable confidence of the band turned into surprise.

It was the posters that first attracted attention: an eight way split of the album cover, the soldier vision of Emile de Antonios in a still from 'The Year Of The Pig' with the legend 'Meat Is Murder' scratched on the soldier's helmet. The posters blew the title huge and diagonal across the complete vision. Commuters virtually 'tripped up' over the words which pulled no punches in all the cities and towns of Britain. The idea was impact and it succeeded. Eight months previously ZTT's Paul Morley had used the XL image factory and Katherine Hamnett to plaster fragments of his prose on to the chests of the nation's youth. The only wastage of effort was that his sloganeering did nothing other than promote 'Frankie Goes To Hollywood' product and cause meaningless provocation along the way. 'Meat Is Murder' opened a nationwide debate and used the power of record promotion to push an idealism still, amazingly, regarded as militant in this country. It was a brave move. The Smiths, who had always taken a leaf out of Factory's books by disguising their visual imagery behind heavy subtlety, now showed a deliberately provocative front.

The music press treated 'Meat Is Murder' with approving caution. Nobody risked showering the album with reams of ecstatic praise: 'Close, but no cigar' became the order of the day. It was too obvious a record to hail as a classic. Most fell in line with the view that The Smiths would one day produce the perfect artifact and that 'Meat Is Murder' was most definitely a step in the right direction. Equally, nobody could find a scrap of positive criticism. There is a whole new world (for The Smiths) within the record. True enough, Morrissey disregarded his original bedsit self pity and began to write from the third person. In short, the album grew out of Morrissey's fevered mind and moved into more journalistic areas.

It also saw Joyce and Rourke emerging as a formidable rhythm section. Whereas previously their contribution had been submerged beneath the power of the front pair, on 'Meat Is Murder' they brought themselves fully into the fray, skilfully powering the music into the subconscious.

The opening thrust of 'The Headmaster Ritual' brought immediate impact and soon became a favourite with all who had bad experiences at school (which is everyone). In effect it was a simple slap at both the school system and the way in which the system actively provokes bullying from pupils or teachers. In actuality it was Morrissey utilising his long sought-after position of power to extract a little revenge, nothing more than "Look at me now, you spineless bastards". To read further is to see Morrissey's message of proof that the school system is not the only way forward. The track which follows, 'Rusholme Ruffians', delves a little further into the past. Based around the most simple of Eddie Cochran chords (deliberate, as the song deals with the atmosphere of the fifties), 'Rusholme Ruffians' sees a young Morrissey wandering around one of those intensely violent travelling fairs and soaking in the absurdities.

This devout sense of humour just manages to rescue the lyrics from falling victim to Morrissey's early teen fixation. That said, it is the perfect complement to 'The Headmaster Ritual'. The tack is reversed during the self explanatory 'I Want The One I Can't Have' which is simple frustration coupled with a rather jagged and repetitive piece of music. This and the following 'What She Said' are the album's only low points. Both songs power through in fairly tuneless fashion.

'That Joke Isn't Funny Anymore' supplies the lifebelt, a misty acoustic ambience which taunts the best of Morrissey's emotions. Again, self explanatory emotions

allow side one to slowly drift away with the repeated line:
"I've seen this happen in other people's lives and now it's
happening in mine". Not, as one first expects, a celebration.
The nature is more of an epitaph.

S ide Two wastes nothing on subtlety. The
opening lines of 'Nowhere Fast' illustrate this:
"I'd like to drop my trousers to the queen, every
sensible child will know what this means…" Oh
for the sadness of reflective socialism. The song careers
through a barrage of the shock tactics of intended cliché.
'Well I Wonder' releases the eardrum pressure and hangs on
the line "Please, keep me in mind" complete with the
synthetic rain of an outsider's view of Manchester. Whatever
comments on the rigours of schooling not exploited on 'The
Headmaster Ritual' reach the surface on 'Barbarism Begins
At Home' although, as the title suggests, this is more
concerned with the wrongs of parental mismanagement.
Harking back to The Smiths' early days, it is another stab at
Victorian virtue: "A crack on the head is what you get for
asking." More simply, a crack on the head is what you get for
acting in a perfectly natural manner. Aggression, in the
Morrissey vision, is something which is both permitted and
to be encouraged in certain circumstances. The question
here, and indeed throughout the entire album, is just when
and where (and to comply with whose moral standard)
natural aggression should be used.

The final title track, a return of the shock tactic,
fades leaving a silence of expectancy, a silence in which
Morrissey inquires, "Right, that's what I think…How about
you?". Indeed, as Paul Du Noyer noted in the *NME*, it might
not make a sausage of difference to your diet but it's
guaranteed to leave a feeling of guilt in your head as you tuck
into that rump steak. Roast beef may never taste the same
again.

I surveyed the area between Manchester's twin
vinyl take-aways (Virgin and HMV), carefully selecting
dowdy individuals with copies of the album under their arms
as they emerged from the doorways. Just one question was
asked to each of the chosen seven: How heavily influenced

are you by the sentiments of groups like The Smiths and do you think that a record like that is capable of causing a drastic change in your attitudes to a subject like vegetarianism?

Shirley Dale, Wilmslow: "I like the music. I'm not a vegetarian although quite a number of my friends are. I can't see this making any difference. It might make a few people think, which is good. The thing is that it's obviously a genuine sentiment and that's why I like The Smiths. It's not, I don't think, just another gimmick. I've not heard that track yet anyway."

Steve Pritchard, Burnage: "No...that's one thing I dislike about The Smiths. They, or rather Morrissey, thinks he's all wise and a sort of father figure. I'm quite capable of making up my own mind on subjects like vegetarianism. I don't want it ramming down my throat. I don't like the title, it's probably done for the right reasons but...well...I'm learning to play guitar and I like Johnny Marr's style. That's why I've bought the record."

Sue Morley, Royton: "It won't change my views. I do have slight vegetarian principles like I think it's disgusting to use animals for luxury things like cosmetics or fur coats but food is a different matter".

John Cole, Skelmersdale: "Morrissey obviously believes in what he is saying and is brave enough to say it whatever the consequences. You've got to admire that. They are the only band in the country who have anything positive to say. You've just got to listen to them. I don't think it will make me a vegetarian but it might make me think about it. If it just makes ten people change their minds then it is worthwhile. Most of my friends will buy this album and we usually waste a lot of time discussing the merits of whatever record we have recently bought, so we may well have a few arguments on whether to eat meat or not. How can that be a bad thing. Also they are the best band in the world."

Mystery couple, (they wouldn't give their names): "They (The Smiths) make music that means something. Morrissey can be a bit of a misery but you can always dance to it. It's just good pop music but with more about it than your average group. What? We are not going to tell you about our eating habits. That's an invasion of privacy, isn't it dear..."

Dave Sayer, Newton Heath: "It's the event of the year. You have got to have this album to er...to stay hip. No, I'm not a vegetarian and it won't make me one but they are perfectly entitled to push their views across through their records. I just like the music. That's all."

So, if our tiny survey is to be considered representative (and I suspect that it is), then 'Meat Is Murder' is generally seen as an honest statement but not one which will cause a drastic change of thinking (or eating) patterns.

Nevertheless, the red clad picture of Morrissey on the cover of *Smash Hits* clutching a 'Meat Is Murder' placard was symbolic of his influence. Selling such statements to thirteen-year-old girls is something which had more than a small measure of the bizarre. The interview inside revolved totally around vegetarianism. The exchange, with *Smash Hits* Tom Hibbert, was as direct as possible within this vehicle.

Hibbert: "Did you approve of the Animal Liberation Front's Mars Bars hoax?"

Morrissey: "Oh yes, completely. I think we have to take these measures now because polite demonstration is pointless. You have to get angry, you have to be violent because otherwise what's the point? There's no point in demonstrating if you don't get any national press, TV or radio...or nobody listens to you or you get beaten up by the Police..."

Unusually harsh words for the Smash Hits world and one imagines waves of rebellious schoolchildren refusing to eat school dinners. Unfortunately, perhaps, it doesn't work that way as most younger teens show a commendable desire to make up their own minds on subjects such as this. At best, 'Meat Is Murder' helped open new fields of debate and, perhaps, intensify the resolve of the already converted.

As abrasive as ever, Morrissey made a appearance on Radio One's *Round Table* where he cut to ribbons practically every recording artist in the country.

"I don't understand Phil Collins and I don't suppose I ever will", said Morrissey, ironically in the week when Phil Collins' 'No Jacket Required' knocked 'Meat Is Murder' off the number one spot.

The most vociferous response to 'Meat Is Murder' stemmed from those in opposition to the statement. Letters stuffed full of anti-Smiths sentiment flooded into the music press offices. One example, from the April issue of *Jamming*, read: "Times change, and fashions move on. Six years ago it was racism, then nuclear disarmament, then the Ethiopian famine and now, animal rights. So Morrissey wants to convert us all to being staunch vegetarians does he? I don't tell him what clothes to wear, why should he tell me what food to eat? I'm really fed up with all these self-righteous musicians telling us what to think and do. If I want to hear about politics, I'll go out and vote. Music is meant to be about escapism, not dreary boring subjects like the miners' strike and animal rights. When Tony Fletcher says the track 'Meat Is Murder' will make you "stall over your bacon sandwich", who does he think he's kidding? Most Smiths fans are good old carnivores and unlikely to give up meat just 'cos Morrissey says so. What's it going to be next? Plant protection? Save the gay black whale? Leave the music to those who enjoy it and the politics to those who'll listen (nobody)." Cathy McCabe, Lincoln.

So, with one LP, Morrissey set himself up as the new Tom Robinson? Not so. The Smiths will never be a band locked into the mechanics of party politics, but if The Smiths are about life then they are about politics. As popular music is an effective soapbox, then people will always use it to express their feelings and quite rightly. That said, it does stimulate a 'rent-a-cause' situation and attach a 'trendy' tag to what are, quite often, extremely serious subjects. It's up to individuals to continue to fight for their beliefs after the trendiness vanishes.

In Manchester 'The Headmaster Ritual' caused its own little storm in a teacup. This became clear after parents began to ring Manchester's Piccadilly Radio in protest over the song's condemnation of their local school system. This led to nothing more than Morrissey's former headmaster making a radio appearance wherein he spoke briefly in defence of the education system before recalling proud remembrances of his former pupil. He seemed to be claiming a slice of the glory; alarming how a splash of fame can twist situations into reverse achievements.

ore absurd was the sight of Johnny Marr in a Sale chip shop buying, wait for it, a steak pie. This caused much concern in the Haçienda. Gone, it seems, are the days when rock stars caused major scandals by being caught with dangerous drugs. A bag full of cocaine is one thing but a *steak pie*?

Similarly, a number of Morrissey's former acquaintances (again, those who were left behind) told tales of how the singer downs many a bottle of wine despite his public image as the complete celibate with a teetotal lifestyle. This is another area of concern for Morrissey. His celibacy and vegetarianism clash violently with the northern working class society he professes to represent. Forty Woodbines, twelve pints, two curries and a porno video a day…he isn't. But many of the most militant of Morrissey attackers most definitely are. Vegetarianism, above all else, is seen to be an affront against a traditional way of life. (In the north, Sundays mean a roast joint, Yorkshire pudding and gravy. It genuinely *is* like that and a statement like 'Meat Is Murder' causes offence to the strictly guarded view of the nice, normal family.) The cry goes out…vegetarians are gay or wimpish.

In *Smash Hits*, Morrissey mused over this feeling. "I can't really think of any reason why vegetarians should be considered effeminate. Why? Because you care about animals? Is that effeminate? Is that a weak trait? It shouldn't be and I think it's a very sad reflection on the human race that it often is."

But it isn't because you care about animals. It's because you refuse to fall into the stereotype view of a 'real man'. That beer swilling, tattooed, sexist monstrosity which is fast heading into extinction anyway.

Nobody really cares if Morrissey is gay or not. Nobody really cares if he chooses not to eat meat. What causes offence is that he merely represents a shifting of values for the mass of young people. These values are not primarily the pursuit of small amounts of money paid in a weekly wage. These values extend well into the boundaries of improbability. This is something which, we are told, is impractical. A bad influence. Which is rock 'n' roll.

Even within the ultra-clean pages of *Smash Hits*, there are a number of bad influences featured every fortnight. What makes The Smiths so different is the amount of thought and reasoning which accompanies every statement. Equally, The Smiths counterparts in the rock field like, say, U2 may make fine music but they shy away to hide behind subtleties of abstract lyricism. Nothing particularly wrong with that, but they avoid the mass of questioning which will obviously follow such strongly opinionated music. It's little wonder that the naturally shy Morrissey often seeks to retreat. That kind of pressure is difficult to bear, however self induced.

but they avoid the mass of questioning which will obviously follow such strongly opinionated music. It's little wonder that the naturally shy Morrissey often seeks to retreat. That kind of pressure is difficult to bear, however self induced.

As 'Meat Is Murder' was steadily devoured and after the initial hysteria had faded away, how did the new music stand in comparison to the angst-ridden image of the early band?

Janice Long: "Their talent has matured and, although I still love the early stuff, everything since has got better and better. Listen to 'Meat Is Murder'. There isn't a duff track on it. Favourites for me, of all Smiths tracks ever? 'How Soon Is Now', 'Please, Please, Please', 'Headmaster Ritual' and 'This Charming Man'."

Interesting to note that the flamboyant Janice only includes one song from 'Meat Is Murder'. That said, after talking to many Smiths fans and close acquaintances, it seems that 'Meat Is Murder' rates as the peak achievement...so far.

By this time, The Smiths had embarked on their most extensive British tour to date. Opening at the Brixton Academy, the tour visited the most gigantic venues in the south before slowly moving northwards and back again to climax at the ultra-prestigious Royal Albert Hall. Critics, amongst them Dave McCullouch (as already mentioned), saw this as the final sell-out. How could The Smiths sink into big time rock and roll and retain their integrity? How can such sentiments retain their edge when rendered from the Royal Albert Hall stage? Who are you going to see tomorrow? The Smiths? Dire Straits? What difference does it make? On the other hand...just how does one escape those trappings?

It's easy to criticise but when an audience grows to this size, there is the responsibility of allowing as many fans as possible to see the shows. To play small venues would invite élitism. Shows for the privileged? This would attract even more criticism. Maybe there is room to use this power of attraction to create a new method of live rock music performance. But this could quite easily turn into farce or pretension. The logistics of a large scale rock show demand certain necessities and, frankly, there is no way round this. I believe The Smiths to be totally innocent of this charge.

Brixton Academy was ecstatic, a classic event. The understandably nervous James took deep breaths and confronted the Smith-hungry audience with their own peculiar brand of folky experimentalism. To Morrissey's satisfaction, they gained a warm response. The Smiths were pleased. They, at least, felt a responsibility towards the hand-picked support band. It's interesting to note that The Smiths were determined to pick the support band themselves regardless of what label they hail under (strangely enough – Factory). It is with worrying regularity that many of today's major tours offer a 'home label' support act as the majors fight desperately to gain attention for their smaller acts. This veers dangerously towards the old method of 'paid' support acts. The Smiths could have received a considerable amount of money by this method and, indeed, were offered a number of more lucrative alternatives. The whole idea would have backfired if The Smiths audience had rejected James.

As for The Smiths themselves, they fell into the enviable routine with natural gusto and confidence, Joyce and Rourke assuming a higher musical profile than ever before. As the music powered into focus, it suddenly seemed much more than a mere backdrop for Morrissey's lyrical diatribes. Morrissey himself, attired in a ripped white shirt and trilby hat, acted out the totally ridiculous spectacle which, somehow, absurdly fitted into the field of pop music. Never was it more obvious just what an unlikely figure Morrissey cut as a pop star. This ungainly fellow, dressed in dishevelled robes and dancing with a curiously lopsided but fetching clumsiness, somehow managed to touch thousands. It was truly the most absurd of happenings.

Dutifully, the press arrived in droves to pay homage to what was obviously the start of the country's number one tour. The most telling accounts were to be seen in the local press whose journalists had gone along on routine reporting assignments and tried to come to terms with the decidely un-pop star look of the performers onstage. The Smiths were completely and hilariously out of the reach of the general press.

Music writers, however, were united in their fervour. "It sends shivers down the spine to think how good the Smiths are. That's nothing on how good they could be, given half a chance. Three albums in a year but they still reek of potential and new ideas," wrote Eleanor Levy in *Record Mirror*.

In *The Guardian* Robin Denselow touched on subjects closer to the heart of this book: "The Smiths may be the most popular band in Britain but the contradictions within this tunefully doomy quartet seem ever more bizarre. On one side there is the odd figure of Morrissey with his doleful voice and intriguing lyrics that offer an orgy of catharsis and sing-a-long confession for those plagued with inadequacies, mixed with horror and fascination with violence. And on the other side there is the backing trio straining at the leash to counter the drifting introspection with their light but impassioned playing."

Cute, but I'd say the effect was of a unity rather than a two-sided battle. That said, the drifting of Morrissey's voice over an unlikely background makes for the most effective twin attack since Yazoo. Interesting to note the apparent 'freshness' of the gig which lasted almost two hours. Traditional they may be by instrumentation, but the way in which they apply their collective noises is unique. This is neither brash, spotty punk nor controlled smoothly executed musicianship but a careful balance which utilises the expertise of the latter and loses none of the instantaneous excitement of the former. But live, for a first time viewer, they can only hope to achieve a possible connection via the actual presentation and general 'sound'. So what makes them so different? What do the audience get from a live show? Basically it is an accessory to the already solid connection between band and fans, a confirmation that the band exist as real working people and a chance for both sides to voice their appreciation of the other. A dual homage and an age old ritual. It is a connection which exists beyond this ritual-meaning. An outsider would find little difference between a Smiths concert and a U2 concert – logistics being what they are: a light show, a mixing desk, guitar/bass/drums and vocals have a limited amount of scope.

But, more importantly, a Smiths gig is merely part of a night out, something to talk about in the pub afterwards. Good as the band may well be, they can't escape the fact that huge gigs are not the most enjoyable of experiences. This doesn't just apply to those who have paid for the event. Barely a week into the tour, Johnny Marr was feeling the strain: "I feel like I'm in The Rolling Stones or any other rock band," he said as the gruelling schedule began to etch away at the excitement generated by that first night. Routine soundcheck-hotel-gig-hotel-travel-hotel always has a dulling effect on performance. This unavoidable routine is a whirlpool through which many an interesting outfit loses all they originally used to gain initial recognition.

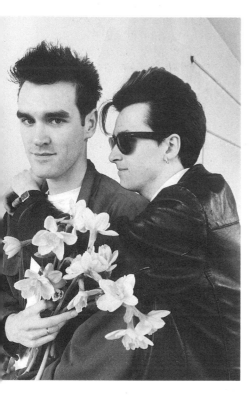

On the one hand we have what appears to be pop star wingeing, but most people would give their right arm to be the principle subjects on a tour of this scale. Nothing is more annoying than when a dole queue fan shells out six pounds for a ticket to a show which is nothing but a huge yawn for the artist involved.

On the other hand…if the artist becomes nothing but a mechanical cog in the constantly revolving schedule, then the show becomes something less than artistic. Yes, these are the very same thoughts which marred the first tour. Just a little more intense and a touch more desperate.

This tour saw The Smiths diving into new areas of complete inaccessibility. Morrissey, in particular, would lock himself away behind a shield of management statements and subsequent verbal minders. Backstage at the Brixton Academy two fans were kicked to the ground while attempting to gain admittance to the dressing room. One thinks back to Morrissey in the early days and wonders why it has to be this way.

This aside, the tour was a success every night. By the time it reached the Manchester Palace it had become the most well documented tour of the year. In Manchester the demand for tickets was so great that they changed hands for upwards of eighty pounds. The security at the Palace was so tight that even the band's ersatz manager, Scott Piering, could not gain admittance for his close acquaintances. The beautifully refurbished Palace was the only upward step the band could make after their previous Manchester appearance at the Free Trade Hall. Essentially Manchester's only outlet for West End musicals, the theatre didn't know what had hit it. A Sunday night of utter madness.

The now 'buzzing' James (a week previously they had consented to allow the *NME* to run their cover story) went into discussion with The Smiths over a proposed filming of James' appearance for release on Factory's video outlet Ikon. Factory were keen to retain the band despite the A & R attention from the majors. It would have been an apparently simple operation involving nothing more than a straight filming of the set. The Smiths, somewhat surprisingly, refused to allow this to happen. Factory were a little nonplussed by the decision. It appeared that The Smiths thought they had given enough exposure to James and that Factory was now taking advantage of the situation. Rough Trade thought that recent press attention for James plus a brilliant performance on *Whistle Test* was stealing a little too much away from the headline act. The Smiths were becoming worried. The truth probably lies somewhere between the two. Once again, The Smiths were not held in high regard in the minds of the Factory élite.

Not surprisingly, the Manchester gig climaxed with a traditional shaking of The Palace foundations. The tour wound onwards and for the performers bored or not, the excitement intensified nightly. By the time they reached The Royal Albert Hall, they were both exhausted and exhilarated. The Albert Hall is regarded as a 'mega-gig' venue and as such is an uncomfortable nod to the future. If they are prepared to move with apparent ease into surroundings of this nature, will they equally find no problems by moving into the Wembley Arenas of this world? How can they possibly control such success?

The Smiths fully admitted that The Albert Hall was a stupidly flash choice of venue. The hall just couldn't cope and after six songs they retreated to the dressing room. A dangerous crush followed a surge at the front of the stage and the security subsequently panicked. As the minutes of silence and confusion unfolded, the crush eased and a visibly shaken band were allowed back onstage. The gig continued but was effectively overshadowed by the possibility of impending disaster and it wasn't until the encores of 'William, It Was Really Nothing', 'Heaven Knows I'm Miserable Now' and 'Barbarism Begins At Home' that they slipped into the comfort of early promise.

Nevertheless, the subsequent press reviews demonstrated that no Smiths backlash was in motion. Both *Melody Maker* and the *NME* remained fiercely loyal. Strange as, at times, Morrissey appears to beg criticism.

Johnny Marr: "Sometimes, when there are three thousand people hanging on every note, I find myself wishing that they were all stood at the bar and facing the other way. Sometimes I wish that we had to work for our reception."

One of the lighter aspects of the tour was the plight of the hamburger salesmen; lighter moment providing you aren't a hamburger salesman, that is. Business was so bad that they moved to more lucrative areas before the shows had even finished.

At the Brixton Academy one stated: "Last night, there can't have been two hundred people at the gig and I sold twice as many burgers and hot dogs than I did today. Today there must have been fifteen hundred people here. The Smiths are definitely a no-go area as far as we are concerned in the future."

No Smiths fan, it seems, would dare to be seen holding the dreaded burger. This resulted in Morrissey being pelted with a pound of sausages at a future gig. As I said, these events verged on the truly bizarre. Meanwhile...

Shakespeare's Sister.

The world was not set alight by the sound of 'Shakespeare's Sister'. The world had expected to be. As the song was not on the album or on any previous release, failure seemed impossible. The Smiths were priming themselves for a spell in the top five. Nobody doubted the chances of this happening. Four weeks later The Smiths were bitterly complaining about Rough Trade's handling of the record. Johnny Marr blamed 'record company stupidity' for the single's comparative failure. Arguments at Rough Trade's headquarters were the talk of the music business.

Morrissey had inspired speculation by his conspicuous non-attendance at the band's post-Albert Hall lig a couple of weeks previously. (For the uninitiated this is a gathering of the privileged few to down cocktails, cause gossip column 'sensations' and generally be seen and pamper the stars of the show).

But 'Shakespeare's Sister' (which took its title from a Virginia Woolf essay on what would have happened if the bard had been female, a different way of looking at women although one has to search hard to find any reference to this in the actual song) was hardly the band's most shining masterwork, merely a jumble of rock and rockabilly plummetting through 129 seconds which fail to motivate the memory cells. Its one claim to fame was that it agitated a sudden outbreak of Northern Soul style dancing in the trendier clubs of Britain. The single had an amazing knack of finishing before you managed to come to terms with it. Subsequently, it failed to build on the extensive Radio One airplay it was given. 'Shakespeare's Sister' reached number seventeen. Many still believed that its position should have been much higher.

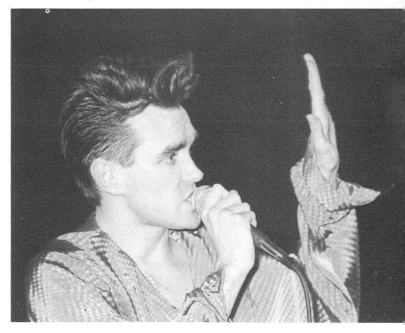

Piccadilly Radio D.J. Tony Michaelides: "I believe it is a terrific record and, without doubt, there was a fault somewhere along the line. It should have been gigantic."

This is exactly the way the band saw it and, when pushed, certain employees of Rough Trade agreed that there had been some kind of promotional foul-up.

However, a letter which appeared in the *NME* illustrated another school of thought. "How can The Smiths blame Rough Trade for 'Shakespeare's Sister' not getting very high in the chart. The fact is that the song did not sell well because, let's face it, it was a bloody awful record..."

In general, most Smiths fans 'tolerated' the record and found it 'all right'. None thought it deserved a higher chart placing.

It did have a most beautiful sleeve, a yellow tint vision of a young Pat Phoenix, a product of Morrissey's youthful Coronation Street obsession. It didn't improve the band's pledge to give value for money. Even the twelve inch, retailing at £2.99, lasted for just two minutes nine seconds. The press, again amazingly, failed to jump on this fact but this was the beginning of the Morrissey press explosion. Nobody wanted to risk losing that interview.

THE MORRISSEY EXPLOSION

"I've seen this happen
in other people's lives
And now it's happening
in mine".

(from 'That Joke Isn't Funny Anymore.)

Those who thought that Morrissey's profile in 1984 was becoming detached from the rest of the band certainly couldn't have appreciated the enormous media attention he generated in spring 1985. If there was, as Morrissey had previously hinted, a certain amount of jealousy within the band then this must have intensified ten-fold as Morrissey captured a limelight which made Boy George seem like a recluse.

In the space of two months (March/April) the singer graced the covers of *NME, Melody Maker, Jamming, Zigzag, Blitz, Smash Hits, Time Out* and many more. He led BBC 2's *Oxford Road Show* on an uneventful wander around his ex-home town of Stretford. He made more gossip column copy than our delightful Princess.

He revelled in the spotlight. For one so shy, he nursed an extraordinary thirst for attention. Some of the interviews he gave were probing and are worth further investigation. The tabloids couldn't quite grasp what they had here. How in the world do you pigeon-hole such an entity?

M orrissey was simply experimenting with the many facets of media attention. The rest of the band appeared perfectly content to let this happen. Initially, following the release of 'Meat Is Murder', Morrissey stated that he had exhausted the conventional format of pop interviews and didn't wish to involve himself in any more. After turning down a *Melody Maker* request on these grounds, editor Allan Jones asked Morrissey for a convenient alternative. As manager Scott Piering was overburdened with similar requests from fanzines, Morrissey came up with the idea of gathering a forum from six or seven of these fanzines. A representative from each travelled to London for a joint interview chaired by Jones, and subsequently published in *Melody Maker*. It was a brilliant tactical move which killed seven birds with one stone, gave The Smiths four pages in *Melody Maker* and gave the fanzines a slice of national exposure.

The questions were indeed a test of Morrissey's resolve. Herewith a sample of the most intriguing moments:

Eat Yourself Fitter: "What's behind the fierce outspokenness against the work ethic in your lyrics?"

Morrissey: "The realities of work, I think. The realities of being in a situation where you can't choose your employment, which is an awful way to be when you don't have any skills and you have to take whatever is dished out...there's nothing worse than having to take what's available. There's nothing worse in life than having no choice, I think. And this is tolerable in all areas except unemployment. When you have to take a job, even if it's a job you can mildly stomach...the fact that you have no choice crushes your enthusiasm for doing the job."

(Which is a hark back to Morrissey's rejection of accepted patterns of life. Leave school, get a job, get married, get a mortgage. The Smiths stand one hundred per cent behind the dismantling of this 'dulling' syndrome).

Eat Yourself Fitter: "Do you think that now you are successful you've merely traded one form of misery for another?"

Morrissey: "No, I don't think so. Virtually everything about the pop industry I detest. I don't feel a part of it to any degree. But that's fine because now we are becoming successful, and I think it's very interesting that The Smiths can survive, nonetheless, even though we all feel this way. So that's unique. But I don't feel absolutely entirely miserable. I *would*, if I couldn't do this."

In general, the inquisition saw Morrissey operating in his perfect role. He was fast becoming the most sought after and most beloved interviewee in Britain. Journalists expected, and often received, quick-fire answers to complex questions. These would often be of a highly important and sensitive nature, transcending the traditional rock interview. Morrissey was elected 'hip-priest' and, as such, was expected to be all wise and all knowing. Carefully, he narrowed this down to opinion, but his was a highly pressurised role where he had to think carefully over every throwaway line. Nobody asked Morrissey about his 'musical influences' any more. A seemingly endless queue of journalists and would-be's formed, all intent on taking the art of rock interviewing into new and deeper areas. All were equally intent on bringing the icon down and thus perpetuating their own careers. Suddenly intelligent rock journalism became a necessity. Significantly, the lightweight *Smash Hits* journalese became out-moded once more.

As such, Morrissey was seen as a lone subversive hope. The tabloids, finding it impossible to compete with this intense copy, reverted to one-line slandering. They saw the early scandals (which they had created) as the prime reason for The Smiths success.

I n a *Time Out* interview with Simon Garfield, Morrissey spoke of this: "They (the tabloids) hound me and it gets very sticky. What makes me more dangerous to them than anybody else is the fact that I lead a somewhat serene and religious lifestyle. I'm not a rock 'n' roll character. I despise drugs. I despise cigarettes. I'm celibate and live a very serene lifestyle. But I'm also making very strong statements lyrically and this is very worrying to authoritarian figures. They can't say that I'm in a druggy haze or soaked in alcohol and that I'll get out of it. They probably think I'm some sex craved monster. But that's okay. They can think what they like. I'm only interested in evidence and they can't produce any evidence to spoil my character."

The politics of politeness became Morrissey's greatest weapon. This peaceable character, dressed down in Levi's and C & A sweaters, polite, nervous, very shy and completely, utterly disarming, would sit with legs crossed, speak in low inoffensive tones, employ the look of a total apologetic office clerk, butter wouldn't melt…and yet display complete integrity and confidence and produce statements like…

"Actually, I despise royalty. I always have done. It's fairy story nonsense, the very idea of their existence in these days when people are dying daily because they don't have enough money to operate one radiator in the house, to me, is immoral. As far as I can see, money spent on royalty is money burnt. I've never met anybody who supports royalty and believe me I have searched. Okay, so there is some deaf and elderly pensioner in Hartlepool who has pictures of Prince Edward pinned on the toilet seat but I know streams of people who can't wait to get rid of them." (*Time Out.* March 7-13th 1985.)

His subversity is effective because he makes sense. The Sex Pistols (who once touched on a similar subject) also made sense, once, but although Johnny Rotten was a wry and clever ambassador for the feeling of the youth, he equally made it perfectly easy for the tabloids to pin him with yobbishness. Not so Morrissey. Morrissey fronts a youthful revolution which isn't locked in tribal chant nor the blank idealism of the sixties. Maybe he represents the fact that youth rebellion has learnt its lesson, that it has returned in a stronger, more considered, more intelligent format. That at last it poses a genuine threat. Maybe.

Morrissey deliberately used his high profile to construct a public figure of some importance. Far away from the usual round of interviews for reasons of record promotion, he was etching his personality into the minds of the readers. To create a persona? He says not. He says (with believable sincerity) it is quite simply a projection of his genuine self. That he is exposing all. That this is a first in the history of popular music. What makes this alarmingly believable is Morrissey's proven shyness. For instance, he finds it almost impossible to speak on the telephone. I checked. He has always been like this. It's not because he is sick and tired of talking to people (which would be understandable), it is because he is truly very, very shy. He just isn't capable of selling a nut to a squirrel. The chances are that this shyness would have naturally prevented him from attaining such a high profile…but Morrissey slipped through the net and the consequences could be devastating. It is Morrissey himself who is being warped, twisted and cheated by the media.

Providing he retains control (which he has so far succeeded in doing), he can play the media and not be affected by the media's idiosyncrasy. Should the media gain control (i.e. should it begin to make Morrissey believe all he reads) then the man may be in danger of losing all to complete blandness, and possibly worse.

That young starlet in the up and coming young writers' guild, Antonella Black (What luck, at last the new Jane Suck) provided half of one of the most interesting games of verbal tennis with Morrissey to date in *Sounds* on April 20 1985. It was also one of the few occasions where the singer's sense of humour was enticed from the shell.

A.B: "What's preventing you from being happy?"

Morrissey: "I don't know. I think it's something to do with the hormones. I haven't a clue."

A.B: "Your neuroses perhaps?"

Morrissey: "Give me a chance to answer the question. Good heavens, that's the first time I've shouted since 1976…I've been in every conceivable situation in human existence."

A.B: "You have had group sex on a rubber mat with a bowl of custard?"

Morrissey: "Daily, it's a terrible yawn."

A.B: "You have starved in a ghetto?"

Morrissey: "I have been in *almost* every conceivable human situation…I've been in almost NO conceivable human situation, come to think of it."

Get the drift? The interview went onwards into a mass of sexual innuendo before Morrissey was removed speedily from young Antonella's reach by his tour manager. This didn't stop the interview from re-surfacing two weeks later in *Zigzag* wherein Morrissey acknowledged his undying erotic passion for leather car seats, amongst other things…all fairly lightweight banter and all revolving, enticingly (?) around Morrissey's underlying eroticism.

Without meaning to fall into pretentious meanderings, it does appear as if Morrissey finally needed a release from his previously closely guarded sexuality. Jovially swapping innuendos which a year earlier would have been seen as bad taste sexism by the singer. As somebody once said, celibacy lies next to orgasm. What Morrissey still can't come to terms with is that now, for some strange reason, hordes of people profess to have fallen in love with him and previous to the band, he often states, no girl ever even took him into consideration. To add to his confusion, he still finds himself sat alone watching television and wondering where all these people are.

The whole plastic notion of a pop star begins to ring the bells of truth. His only saving grace is his undying belief in the melodramatic.

Morrissey takes interviews extremely seriously, perhaps over-analysing the final product. (He taped the Antonella interview(s) for his own scrutiny). He obviously enjoys the medium and, at times, it has proved to be a superior form of communication than the records themselves. On vinyl, he is separated, safe, subtle and simply, a one-sided statement. In interview, he is exposed, pressured and forced to qualify everything.

More importantly, he is not in control of the final product. This causes a positive paranoia. It also causes lucrative publicity *and* a scapegoat, but that's another story. He enjoys the paranoia and, indeed, it fuels his interest. However, there have been times where he has no control at all and this is where he slips into panic.

One of Britain's finest music journalists, the sadly redundant Nick Kent, decided to re-enter the world of journalism via a retrospective on the one group he found worthy, The Smiths. Indeed a tremendous compliment to the band, and manager Scott Piering welcomed the exercise. Morrissey however, hearing of Kent's archaeological digging into his past, completely panicked and demanded to see the results prior to publication. Sensing an improvement of story, Kent agreed even though nothing of distaste was uncovered. The resultant article adopted a slightly different base subject, that of Morrissey's neurosis. Hence, the obsessive nature of the man weighted the article towards the angle that Morrissey had originally feared. The piece was written in good taste but couldn't help but leave the reader wondering just what made Morrissey so paranoid. No smoke without fire?

Morrissey had another score to settle. He still considered himself something of a failed journalist (*NME* amongst others, had turned him down five times in the early years) and he often expressed a desire to use his new found influence to move into spasmodic fits of journalese. Effectively, he interviewed his childhood heroine Pat Phoenix for *Blitz*. The ratings competition being what it is, *Blitz* put Morrissey on the cover of the magazine when, of course, it should have been graced by the familiar features of Elsie Tanner. Although the piece was a well balanced probe into the Phoenix career (and an immensely interesting career it is too), one was left with the feeling that she wouldn't have been there had it not been for the status of her interviewer. Just how Morrissey will come to terms with this problem is a matter for some speculation. Maybe he is content just to pay tribute to his personal media icons. Maybe he is merely realising the ambitions of a fan.

"We are the best band in the world. There is nobody better." (Andy Rourke.)

"We are the only truly controversial band of the eighties." (Johnny Marr.)

The Smiths have always laid great claims to their art. All four band members share the belief that nobody can match the measure of commitment and unity to be found within The Smiths. Possibly this is a direct result of the speed of their ascent. (Remember, none of The Smiths naïve early predictions failed to materialise). Both The Smiths' claims to greatness plus their collective decision making have evolved into fruition with perfect symmetry. This has strengthened their unity and imposed an almost over-bearing fear of breaking the chain. So, as the individual trust strengthens, the band's reputation as stubborn unpredictables intensifies. Their move away from video, while strengthening a resolve with the fans, has been strongly criticised within business circles. To a certain extent this is proof of their integrity. There are occasions, though, when their admirable arrogance serves to closet the band behind a mystique bordering on élitism.

The Nick Kent episode is a case in point. They have become the most inaccessible band in the music business. They tend to pick and choose their interviewers. They hide behind a wall of friendly but hard line management. To give them the benefit of the doubt, this may well be necessitated by their unique position, but at times it appears alarmingly like arrogant behaviour. Mike Joyce was incredibly upset at being ignored in the Nick Kent article. However, considering the tightly controlled aloofness and the fact that Joyce (whose contributions in a musical capacity are not in doubt) has led a deliberately low profile, one cannot blame Kent for the omission. This is a problem which the band themselves could easily solve by restructuring their media policy. This aloofness is crucially important in the context of a band completely sold by the sadness of being disregarded. (The aloofness exists. When I first approached The Smiths in regard to this book, although treated with sympathy from their manager, I was waved aside without so much as an acknowledgement. Although used to the scorn of pop stars, I was saddened that The Smiths should act in this way). Earlier, Dave McCullouch stated that, although this was always the case, it didn't have to be. The Smiths showed early promise of breaking traditions, but failed.

But is it avoidable? Can we really expect them to retain the same way of thinking they had as penniless hopefuls, and if they did wouldn't that simply be an insipid patronisation? It is too much to expect musicians to deliberately cast aside the fringe benefits of success. Equally, you can't expect a workable accessibility. With so many journalists wishing to talk with Morrissey, Marr, Rourke and Joyce, surely they have no alternative but to step back and carefully choose their outlets. Even amid the most carefully documented press articles, minor irrelevances are exaggerated into major sweeping testimonies of the band's incapabilities.

An example of this occurred in the Nick Kent piece where Geoff Travis described a sardonic and disgruntled Mark E. Smith antagonising a visibly shaken Morrissey by insisting on calling him 'Steven'. The truth is that Mark has always known him as Steven and naturally found it ridiculous to change to Morrissey. Considering this, the explosion of the most minor points, it isn't difficult to understand why a seemingly pointless paranoia affects the band's every discourse.

But, if they can't break the star system, if it is impossible for a band of this stature to remain in an 'ordinary existence' (although it must be stated that New Order deliberately unglamorise their existence, wisely slowing down their schedules and viciously guarding their faceless media presence. New Order sell tremendous amounts of records *and* walk freely along the streets of Manchester) then wouldn't it be possible for the band to break rock 'n' roll traditions by providing alternatives to the old rock show format?

Many people expect this of The Smiths. Because of the nature of their following, they are still categorised as an 'alternative' outfit. They are pictured next to The Cocteau Twins and Cabaret Voltaire. They are seen as a revolutionary force and as such, should act accordingly. The problem is that this often encourages nothing more than mere farce. The entire ZTT organisation drew up a blueprint for world domination which was a product of the desire to change the pop star syndrome. Good intentions aside, ZTT merely epitomised the medium it professed to hate. It just didn't work.

The Smiths never set out to change anything. The nature of their format is proof of their desire to play the game. The Smiths believe that the sentiments they express are unique and that the music is good enough to cause a general improvement by its sheer excellence. Whether you comply with their claims to being the sole centre of musical importance or not, nobody can say that The Smiths haven't, so far, fulfilled their promise.

But 'Meat Is Murder' marked the end of The
Smiths as we know them. The story continues but the band
have no choice but to move into international areas. This
DEMANDS change but if any band can make this
transformation AND keep their original sense of humility,
then it is The Smiths. The so-called 'bland out' area of
America beckons. The Smiths, although already troubled by
contradictions, still TRY to hold true to those early values.
They just could be the first band in history to sell genuine
English music to the Americans. In Spring '85, preparing for
this onslaught with experimental dates in Spain, one thing
seemed significant. They recorded their new demos not
under the blazing summery affluence of a Compass Point but
in the rundown but equally effective ruins of Out Of The
Blue, an eight track studio in the rat-infested decay of
Ancoats, Manchester.

It seemed the perfect finish to the best story in
modern rock. Somehow, the vision of Morrissey, Marr,
Joyce and Rourke driving Porsches down the Seven Sisters
Road and heading for an evening's ligging at The Camden
Palace, still seems like an impossible nightmare.

Time will tell.

Paint a Vulgar Picture

It was Saturday night at Manchester's vibrant International Club. Seven hundred serious haircuts gathered to pay homage to Liverpool's wild and intelligently wacky Pink Industry, the band led by the individualistic Jayne Casey, fashion queen, Mother Superior and friend of Morrissey.

Pink Industry had just released a single; a rare event to say the least. 'What I Wouldn't Give', besides being utterly forgettable, contained the interesting line, 'There's my Smiths' tapes you never wanted to hear/ Throw them away/Morrissey in the bin.'

The sleeve of this precocious little ditty depicted an impassioned Morrissey (is there any other kind?) gazing upwards into an apparently divine light, no doubt praying for greater record sales. This rather tenuous Morrissey connection managed to gain pockets of press coverage that would otherwise have been wasted on Bananarama or something equally appalling. Whatever, the seven hundred had gathered in earnest and, just prior to the band's flamboyant saunter on to the stage, the International doors were flung open in dramatic fashion. In swayed the pop star, assisted by his Irish minder. He pushed hurriedly through the bar area and located himself directly beneath the mixing desk where, hiding shyly behind the cavorting dance floor bodies, he would attract the minimum of attention.

The Morrissey Problem became apparent in The International that night. Many haircuts aimed themselves towards him, peering, probing, intruding.

"Is that Morrissey, no, his hair's too short. I tell you it is . . . it IS."

A fanzine editor, noting Morrissey's attendance, ploughed through the startled dancers and began to harangue our hero. Behind him a photographer leapt into action and flash after flash turned the normally darkened corner of The International into an impromptu photo call. The minder's hand grasped the photographer's shoulder. His voice rasped, firm but polite.

"Don't you think you've taken enough pictures?" The photographer retired.

Pink Industry played on, rather ineffectively as it happened. Four songs into the set the dark figures of Morrissey and minder were seen to leave the building.

August 1985 was a strange time for The Smiths. Disappointed with Rough Trade's handling of their latest single 'That Joke Isn't Funny Anymore', the band spent a month exploring America, the land that would hold the key to their future. On his return, Morrissey immediately appeared, mean and moody, on the cover of *Record Mirror* with the the word FAKE stencilled into his neck in biro. To the paper's Eleanor Levy, he spoke of America.

"It was very hysterical, very wild, very passionate, very moving. All those things people never believe. It was really quite stunning, even for me, to see it happen. It's quite difficult. When you play concerts in America which are highly successful, it really colours your vision of the entire country. You're quite reluctant to think of the bad points because suddenly it seems like the most perfect patch of land on this planet. I have been there

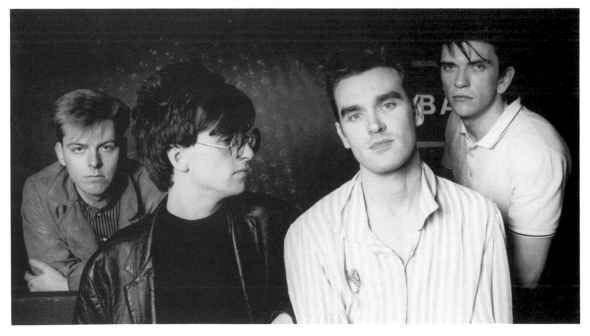

many times and had many unshakeable criticisms, which now have, of course, been shaken.''

Thus spoke a euphoric, besotted Morrissey. The voice of a man in love with a massive and, it would seem, openly welcoming market. Still, the crux of this particular and oddly poignant interview would become evident with the flippant and pointed question, ''Are you making lots of money now?'' With baited breath, we scanned for his answer.

''No, which, I think, is the crux of the present dilemma. I'm still too acquainted with the whole aspect of poverty. I personally work 24 hours every single day of every week, relentlessly, and the dividends in that area certainly don't pay off. In artistic ways they do because the records are successful but I'm tired of being broke, very tired of that, and it's especially hurtful when you meet so many in the industry who don't quite have your status but are laughably rich.''

Morrissey was obviously peeved at The Smiths continued existence as a relatively small 'cottage industry'. The independent ethic they had courted so successfully

since their conception was beginning to fall hopelessly apart. As The Smiths grew in commercial stature, so they encountered more and more professional people, especially in America, and these people constantly told the band to think big, to think mega, to evolve into a major international unit. It was quite obvious that The Smiths, despite the continued artistic success, were just not in any position to think, or indeed to act, big on an international scale. They watched with grave concern the formidable ascent of U2. Although The Smiths clearly regarded themselves as being the better unit, they couldn't hope to compete with U2 on a commercial basis and to the ambitious egos of Morrissey, Marr, Joyce and Rourke, this seemed unacceptable.

Morrissey: ''On all instances when it's left to The Smiths alone, we are unbeatable. I find when we have to rely on others we always seem to be behind everyone else. There's only so much you can cling to – your credibility, your belief in small cottage industries – whatever. You have to be realistic.

"A lot of people say 'You ARE big, you ARE heard, you do have your army of apostles. What are you complaining about?' But I'm in there every day and I'm the one who knows that the profile we have on radio and television should be higher. But I still believe The Smiths can become the most successful force in music . . . "

Have you noticed anything? We've been quoting Morrissey repeatedly from a *Record Mirror* interview and he hasn't been talking about the pain of youth, the imagery of sixties films or the perception of Oscar Wilde. In fact, he hadn't been talking on aesthetic terms at all. His frustration and anger had become angled towards the peculiar career situation of The Smiths, a position that had now grown into one of the most intriguing paradoxes in the history of rock. The irony of The Smiths had become strange and was growing stranger.

It was 'How Soon Is Now' that had initially made the serious inroads into a vast American audience. Before this single, the rather distanced US rock press failed to probe deeply into the phenomenon of The Smiths and had constantly referred to them as some kind of whacko gay outfit, English eccentrics playing lightweight rock. But

'How Soon Is Now', fuelled by an unsolicited US video, kindly supplied by Sire Records out of necessity for MTV, catapulted The Smiths into the hearts and minds of hungry anglophiles.

But, back in England, The Smiths felt unsettled and just a little paranoid. Communications between them and Rough Trade came to a standstill as they prepared to undertake a short Scottish tour, and from this odd situation a strange story came to light. The Smiths invited Rough Trade stablemates Easterhouse to act as support for the tour. This wasn't surprising, for not only were Easterhouse Rough Trade's 'band most likely', they were also close personal friends of The Smiths. Nevertheless, the chance to perform before large Smiths crowds was an exciting opportunity for Easterhouse and they set about rehearsing in earnest.

But as The Smiths were advised to sever all contacts with Rough Trade, they decided to drop Easterhouse from the tour. The problem was that nobody from The Smiths camp was prepared to actually inform the band of this decision, and it was left to Easterhouse manager John Barrett to discover the sad truth almost by accident. Needless to say, Easterhouse were greatly upset, not by the loss of the tour, but by The Smiths apparent lack of concern for them.

As it happened, the entire episode was resolved after The Smiths decided to reopen communications with the label and a somewhat confused Easterhouse were invited back on to the Scottish tour.

Back in Manchester a glossy fanzine called

Muze had picked up on this story and published a naively frivolous little article which dared to question the somewhat confused ethical position of the band. The article wasn't particularly poignant but it did, in places, slide too near to home and too close to the bone. One line, buried near the article's conclusion, caused a great deal of stress within The Smiths' ranks.

"Recent reports of The Smiths damaging the prospective careers of smaller outfits with actions aimed in pure spite at Rough Trade, hardly inspire confidence." A strange and, to those unaware of the Easterhouse situation, ambiguous line which saw Morrissey running for the shelter of his lawyer, Alexis Grower.

o, one fine morning the magazine's publisher and feature writer received a notice informing them that Steven Morrissey and Johnny Marr were proceeding with an action for defamation of character. It seemed bizarre that a band plagued by such huge problems on an international scale should wish to waste their time attempting to sue a small time and, to be frank, penniless local magazine. Now, *Muze* magazine may not have been a high profile organisation but it did provide a much needed platform for the flourishing Manchester rock scene. To see this platform threatened by a mere Smiths' power game, hardly proved good PR for the band and a degree of bad feeling began to boil away in their home city.

The irony was that The Smiths were objecting to an article which suggested that they had become governed by power and finance with an action that was itself a display of power and finance. A report on this peculiar state of loggerheads in the high powered but ill-fated *Hit* magazine hardly eased The Smiths' credibility problem. But at least the rift with Rough Trade appeared to have been solved. A news snippet in *Sounds* seemed to put the situation succinctly into perspective:

"The Smiths, despite inaccurate rumours by one music paper last week, are not leaving Rough Trade – for the time being at least. The stormy relationship with the label has once again been calmed and the band begin recording their fourth album, and a new single, due for release in 1985, this week. Morrissey and the lads were apparently miffed that their last two singles weren't as successful as they had hoped. The choice of the first ('Shakespeare's Sister') and the timing of the second ('That Joke Isn't Funny Anymore'), already available on 'Meat Is Murder', coupled with a lack of airplay were given as reasons for their failure. The fact that the band refuse to do videos and that very little TV promotion was given to these singles didn't help either. Life goes on however, and the band have this week announced a series of Scottish dates. The support, on all dates, will be Easterhouse."

Just prior to the Scottish tour, The Smiths did indeed release a single. Entitled 'The Boy With The Thorn

In His Side', it saw Morrissey's deliberately obvious autobiographical lyric sliding neatly over to flow from Marr's continually inventive mind. It was cute, clever and intelligent, as always. It wasn't designed to attract new listeners, however, for Morrissey's lyric remained both maudlin and frivolous. The single sleeve followed in the band's finer traditions by featuring the great Truman Capote, as captured by the lens of Cecil Beaton.

And, as always, The Smiths were awash in controversy. At Heaton Park in Manchester a supposedly huge anti-heroin open air concert was being planned. The organisers had already begun to promise a strong local bill topped by the two biggest attractions in Manchester at the time, The Chameleons and, of course, The Smiths. This came as a surprise to the band as they had never agreed to play the concert at all and they immediately issued a statement to this effect, fearing that many of their fans were being lured into buying tickets for a Smiths free event. As it turned out, the Heaton Park anti-heroin event was a disaster. The eventual headliners, believe it or not, were Mud.

Still, the troubles continued. The Smiths were booked to appear on Wogan. It was a Friday evening and Marr, Joyce and Rourke dutifully arrived in London expecting to play. Unfortunately Morrissey, without telling the rest of the band, returned to Manchester and the show was cancelled. Curiously, this act of defiance on Morrissey's behalf was, according to the following week's *NME*, " . . . in the hands of lawyers."

Still, amid all manner of rumour, the Smiths/Easterhouse Scottish tour commenced at Irvine Magnum Leisure Centre on September 22. The band performed at the very peak of their live power and the volatile Scottish crowds responded accordingly.

The Glasgow Barrowlands gig was captured, rather strangely, on Channel 4's The Tube. This saw a live rendition of 'Meat Is Murder' spliced with snippets of wholly pretentious banter between Morrissey and Margi Clarke, fresh from her suitably brash role in *Letter To Brezhnev*.

"Oh Margox, Margox. A television luminary from the late seventies," quoth Morrissey. A statement that, to viewers from outside the north west of England, must have seemed bewildering. Morrissey was referring to Margi Clarke's former persona, Margox, and her highly unskilled local television work for Granada, when she presented a late seventies what's on show. This is interesting because Morrissey was referring back to his days spent in hopeless fandom when he practically worshipped everything that moved within the media. What's more, he obviously still elevated those early influences above and beyond their deserved stature. In the north west, it was astonishing to see this superstar, namely

Morrissey, worshipping this formerly dreadful local TV presenter. Thankfully, Margi Clarke had evolved from her modest beginnings into a very fine actress indeed.

On October 9, *Smash Hits* published what must be regarded as the strangest pop cover story of all time, an interview, conducted by the experienced Ian Cranna, with Morrissey and Pete Burns, and headlined 'The Very Odd Couple'. Throughout the land, gullible 13-year-olds would gasp in awe at the revelations laid before them. Preceding the interview, a lush, blue photo of a pouting Burns was captioned with a brief quotation: "If I hear Morrissey's down or depressed, I'll send him a bunch of flowers. He's *anybody's* for a lupin . . . " Oh what camp comedy! Acceptable in many corners of the media, but in *Smash Hits*? The idea was to document, nay, investigate the recent friendship between the two pop icons. It seemed oddly perverse, in a humorous kind of way.

Pete Burns: "I feel a very strong affinity with him, almost a brotherly thing. We've got a lot in common, we don't blend in on the showbiz party circuit . . . "

Morrissey: "Peter is so detached from the pantomime element of the whole industry and the whole party ethic and so are The Smiths."

(Now this struck me as odd. Pete Burns, who may well be an admirable and likeable character, has always struck me as being the embodiment of music business sycophancy.)

Pete Burns: "I always cheer you up, don't I?"

Morrissey: "He sent me 26 roses when it was my birthday and I sent him 48 naked sailors."

Silly camp posing for the nation's spotty youngsters? Two paragraphs later things turned into wonderful sarcasm.

Morrissey: "Specifically the first time 'You Spin Me Round' was on Top Of The Pops . . . that was just barbaric, it was demonic. 'You Spin Me Round' is a hallmark in British music, it will never date."

Pete Burns: "You provocative little minx, you."

Now was that weird, or what. Apparently, The Smiths hated the article when it appeared. I met Ian Cranna a couple of months later. "It did make Morrissey and Burns look like Hinge and Brackett," he admitted.

One month later, The Smiths completed the recording of their third album, 'The Queen Is Dead'. However, the problems between The Smiths and Rough Trade were beginning to climax and, fuelled by the motivation of lawyer Alexis Grower, The Smiths enforced a renegotiation of their Rough Trade contract. This would push the release of 'The Queen Is Dead' back six months.

'And now I know how
Joan of Arc felt'.

In January 1986, The Smiths involved themselves, however tentatively, in the Red Wedge Tour. Morrissey reluctantly made the odd appearance (although he would later disassociate himself from the organisation). Initially it was just Marr and Rourke appearing with Billy Bragg but in Newcastle Morrissey and Joyce consented and a short Smiths set was performed. In many respects the Red Wedge Tour must have helped alleviate some of the frustration and downright weirdness that was bubbling away in Smithdom. With their album completed and, due to legal problems, on ice, The Smiths found themselves in a state of dangerous inactivity. Speaking about this period sometime later to *Record Mirror*'s Eleanor Levy Johnny Marr seemed reflective, in an optimistic kind of way.

"I didn't realise the kind of effect the lay off because of the court case would have on us. We were just deprived of doing what we do - just going in the studio and making records. We'd finished the LP in November and were pretty frustrated about that not coming out. It took

ages to dawn on me that I had to find something else to do with my time other than music. To try to lead a normal life didn't work at all.

"It was so frustrating. Me and Phil, the roadie, even went on this midnight jaunt from Manchester to Guildford to try to steal the master tapes of the LP. It got really silly. We drove all the way down in the snow but they caught us and said we couldn't have them; not surprisingly I suppose."

The short Irish tour which followed proved to be a major turning point in the career of the band. According to Marr, "Two of the gigs were great, one of them wasn't." Hardly an in depth account of what actually went on behind the scenes. For on their return from Ireland, Andy Rourke was sacked.

Marr: "When we got back from Ireland, I

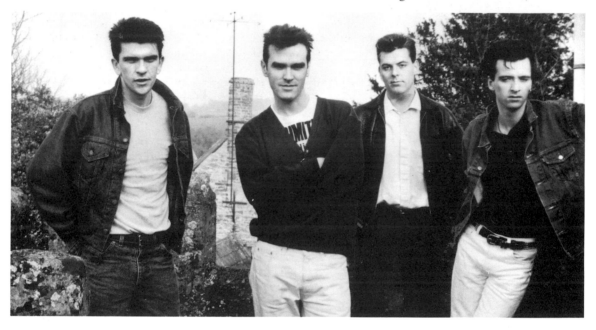

realised I wanted another guitar player. I didn't really need too much time to think about it, I just instinctively knew. We told him to sling his hook . . . then a week later he got busted."

No reason was given for the departure of Rourke at the time, and this only served to intensify speculation. For starters, there was Rourke's well known problem with heroin which had always grated against Morrissey's concept of the band being vegetarian, celibate and literary. Although it must be stated that The Smiths on the road have never corresponded neatly with any 'new man' image. Many said that Morrissey had always objected to Rourke's drug problem and a breakdown of communications on the Irish tour resulted in Marr finally deserting his old school friend to side with old Mozzer.

Rourke's replacement was the young Craig

Gannon, a whizz-kid guitarist of hedonistic bent and formerly with Aztec Camera, The Bluebells and The Colourfield. Gannon was an odd choice although few people picked up on the seemingly obvious fact that he was a rhythm guitarist and not a bass player. To add to the confusion, a month later, Rourke rejoined and the new, hard, heavy, five-piece Smiths were born.

Then there was yet another dispute between the band and Rough Trade supremo, Geoff Travis. On choosing a pre-album single, Travis had opted for 'There Is A Light' which was, frankly, the obvious choice. Johnny Marr had other ideas. He demanded that the single should be 'Big Mouth Strikes Again'. Morrissey dithered between the two.

Many people still believe that Travis was right and 'There Was A Light' would have lodged in the top three. However, it was easy to see why Marr was so keen on 'Big Mouth Strikes Again'. The song held an anthemic 'Smiths are back' feel and contained the finest uptempo guitar work Marr had produced thus far.

On May 3 the writer responsible for the offending *Muze* magazine article, who was still at this point being threatened with legal action from the band, collected the post at his home in Hyde, Cheshire. One letter stood out from the rest. It was addressed to THE FRIED EGG OF ROCK 'N'ROLL and written in the scrawly childlike handwriting that so often accompanied humorous dispatches from the house of Morrissey. Inside the envelope was a postcard depicting the sleeve of The Smiths' forthcoming 'Queen Is Dead' album. On the reverse, more scrawled words said, HALEBARNS 6, HYDE 0.

One week later another such envelope popped mysteriously through the letter box, this time addressed to STAR OF STAGE, SCREEN AND TRAMPOLINE. The envelope contained a 'Big Mouth Strikes Again' label with the words AND SO SAY ALL OF US scrawled strangely

on the other side. The writer filed the exhibit for future reference, happy that court case or no court case, the pop star in question had a sense of humour.

The Smiths appeared on The Tube complete with both Gannon and Rourke. They seemed relaxed, confident and powerful, perhaps relieved to find themselves once again working, once again releasing

records. On Whistle Test they played live to a dead studio, previewing the album with a frivolous snippet, 'Vicar In A Tutu' and, of course, 'Big Mouth Strikes Again'. There was something overwhelmingly assured about this brief appearance. Like any band on the verge of defying all the odds by releasing their finest music to date, just when the public least expected it, they were joyously arrogant.

On July 7 Morrissey appeared shyly on the cover of the *NME*. Significantly there was no headline, a sure sign that the readers would need no prompting in order to recognise the feeling of 'event' that surrounded a Morrissey interview in the *NME*. In one sense, the paper was Morrissey's home.

The interview, conducted by Ian Pye, appeared one week before the release of the album. It would have been better placed a couple of weeks later; at least the readers would have been familiar with the mood and pace of the album.

Pye: "Let's talk about the album."

Morrissey: "Why, for heaven's sake?"

For weeks prior to this, provincial and national newspapers had been expressing their outrage at the title of the album. Not surprisingly, The Smiths were hailed as

anti-monarchists and anarchists. At a later date, Morrissey would conclude that he, "Never anticipated any outrage." Frankly, I cannot believe this. To call your album 'The Queen Is Dead', is to deliberately court controversy with the monarchy-soaked tabloids. A statement from the heart or a mere publicity stunt?

The *NME* interview saw Morrissey eloquent in his condemnation of the monarchy. "I don't want to attack the monarchy in a sort of beer monster way," he stated, rather oddly.

"The whole thing seems a joke, a hideous joke. We don't believe in leprechauns so why should we believe in The Queen? And when one looks at the individuals within the Royal Family, they are so magnificently, unaccountably and unpardonably boring. I mean, Diana herself has never in her lifetime uttered one statement that has been of any use to any member of the human race."

Stirring stuff, and it undoubtedly struck a chord with those who were sick to the back teeth with the royalty in the tabloids. In this respect, Morrissey was on safe ground and, it seemed, no one from *The Sun* reads the *NME*.

One week later 'The Queen Is Dead' came to rest majestically on the record counters. It received universally ecstatic reviews, and deservedly so. It seemed like a thousand years had lapsed since 'Meat Is Murder' and how refreshing it was, how exciting to place the record clumsily on the turntable for the first time to be faced with the full frontal body blow that is the title track. The Smiths may well have attained a state of parody but, amazingly, it didn't matter. Even the parody was gloriously entertaining.

'And so I broke into the palace, with a sponge and a rusty spanner. She said, I know you and you cannot sing, I said, that's nothing, you should hear me play pianer.' (From 'The Queen Is Dead'.)

And as that line emitted from the speakers, several thousand Levi-clad youths walked towards their bedroom Dansettes in a state of disbelief, flipping the needle back a quarter of an inch, in order to catch the line for a second time. But if the new listeners were amazed by that piece of flippancy, then there was more to come.

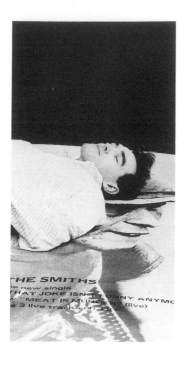

'Fame, fame, fatal fame. It can play hideous tricks on the brain. Still I'd rather be famous than righteous or holy, anyday, anyday, anyday.' One line from 'Frankly Mr Shankly', a vindictive slab of sarcasm aimed directly at the fevered brow of Geoff Travis.

'I Know It's Over' effectively deepened the album. A heartfelt lament and positive proof that Morrissey's voice is indeed a valuable instrument. The Queen was wrong, he *can* sing. 'Never Had No One Never' was a filler, designer Smiths, and worryingly disposable. Thankfully the downward trend stopped at 'Cemetery Gates', an absurdly overstated flash of self parody, immensely pretentious but laughably so, hilariously so. Within this trickle of a song, Morrissey defends his much maligned plagiarism with a comical air of one who considers himself, quite rightly, to be above such charges.

Side two opens with the two singles, 'Big Mouth Strikes Again' and 'The Boy With The Thorn In His Side'. I have to disagree with Adrian Thrills in the *NME* who labelled them as weak and below par. The damage to The Smiths' run of singles was done, not by these two, but the previous 45s, 'Shakespeare's Sister' and 'That Joke Isn't Funny Anymore.'

'Vicar In A Tutu' was pure Carry On camp, an unashamedly silly romp, throwing the listener off balance and hardly in a fit state to take in 'There Is A Light That Never Goes Out', the true pinnacle of the album and the track that, if Mr Shankly had had his way, would have been a classic single. 'There Is A Light' married whimsical comedy with suicidal emotion, in the finest tradition of manic Morrissey. The album closed with 'Some Girls Are Bigger Than Others', utterly frivolous, wonderfully hypnotic. I played it to my mother and she stared at me in total disbelief. That's got to be the mark of good rock 'n' roll.

'As Anthony said to Cleopatra, as he opened a crate of ale, some girls are bigger than others, some girls' mothers are bigger than other girls' mothers . . . ' Indeed.

sixteen

Hang The DJ

I t was July 1986 and the great god of the Manchester music scene, Factory Records supremo Tony Wilson said, "Let there be nostalgia," and indeed the entire city was swamped with punk nostalgia.

Factory Records created and organised The Festival Of The Tenth Summer, a series of 10 events designed to celebrate the tenth anniversary of punk. The events would culminate in a day of worship at Manchester's huge G-Mex centre, where practically every Manchester luminary would appear. The Smiths, of course, were the strongest draw on a bill of unprecedented complexity.

The backstage area at G-Mex was awash with unadulterated sycophancy. Swollen egos battled meaninglessly with a security system which did its level best, but the organisational problems were almost overwhelming. The Smiths were not helping this cause. Even as the day began, rumours were rife that the band had refused to play. Later, in *City Life* magazine, Morrissey would speak of the backstage situation.

"I hoped that the atmosphere backstage wouldn't be as I had imagined, which was the typical Manchester iciness. I found it very abstract. I think it was probably a little too much for the people backstage to deal

with, it just seemed so unreal. All these people and all this musical history of Manchester, all these people together and, although I'm sure they had each other in mind, actually facing these people is very odd. Very strange. It was difficult because the venue was difficult. I'm not really sure whether it happened. I didn't feel any sense of unity, or celebration. Certainly not backstage. Maybe it's just me, I don't know. Maybe it's just the way people behaved towards me. I don't know. Nobody put their arms around me and said, 'Isn't this wonderful?'"

Well, they wouldn't, would they? Nobody would want to be seen crawling to or even making sycophantic noises with Morrissey, of all people. That is the crux of his problem. He has been banished from the real world, we don't allow him to even glimpse at it any more. He may not be the biggest pop star in the world but he's certainly the most unapproachable. The relationship Morrissey conveys through his music is both intimate and intense. Who, though, in the sussed world of professional backstage liggers at G-Mex, would admit to having this relationship with a pop star? That is, in cynical music biz-speak, a punter-ish thing to do. Therefore, at G-Mex, Morrissey was ignored.

The gig was weird but The Smiths, The Fall and New Order were all great. I don't think anyone would argue though, that the true stars of the event came on mid bill, at 6.30pm. It was a strange moment. The time of The Smiths' appearance had not been fully publicised yet, as the strains of Prokoviev's 'Romeo And Juliet' filled the hall, the atmosphere in G-Mex became as intense as Old Trafford on a rare day of victory. Minutes later, 'Big Mouth Strikes Again' filled the ex-railway station with intelligent energy and Morrissey,

dressed in untrendy white, swirled and twirled to the glory of it all. By the time we reached the encore, a stunning 'I Know It's Over', 12 thousand people had been smacked into moronic submission. Even so, the feeling that The Smiths were somehow aloof, somehow estranged from the celebrations, remained prevalent. The Smiths had evolved without the help of Factory. Years previously, Morrissey had invited Tony Wilson round to his house to play him a demo tape. Wilson had declined. This odd refusal seemed to be massively significant at G-Mex, where The Smiths acted as conquering outsiders. The Festival Of The Tenth Summer finished in weirdness. The sycophantic dream of Tony Wilson, Paul Morley and a thousand other Mancunians had been eclipsed by this unique mob, The Smiths.

'Panic', the single, edged its way onto the radio playlists; strange really as 'Panic', the single, was aimed directly at the heart of Radio One idiocy. I heard Steve

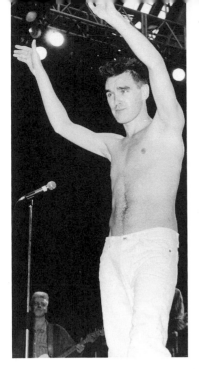

Wright play it once and the irony was almost overwhelming.

'Because the music that they constantly play, it says nothing to me about my life.'

The single was too short, too light and too throwaway. 'Panic' should have been produced heavy and hard, lush and deep. It should have been anthemic instead of light and poppy. I honestly believe that The Smiths, with 'Panic', wasted an opportunity to subvert our beloved mainstream radio playlists. Nevertheless, the single would soon see the band tumbling headfirst into yet another controversy.

On September 27, 1986, there appeared an interview with Morrissey conducted by fellow Mancunian, Frank Owen. Now Owen shared a similar cultural background to Morrissey – he used to hang around the same clubs, he was singer with the post punk band Manicured Noise, a band often linked with Morrissey's beloved Ludus, and the feature was a fascinating if bewildering jumble of nostalgic bonhomie. However, any kind of kinship which may have been struck up was completely ruined by Owen's insistence that 'Panic' was an anti-black music song. True enough, Morrissey fell into a rant which denounced the likes of Whitney Houston, Stevie Wonder and Diana Ross, fair comment in my opinion, but the implication of underlying racism, which the Owen piece implied, wasn't deserved. Still, it must be stated that a man as profoundly outspoken as Morrissey (remember his line, 'All reggae is vile'?) must occasionally find himself in trouble.

The Smiths were not happy with the *Melody Maker* piece and, not surprisingly, more court proceedings began to take place. The relationship between the band and the paper has never completely recovered.

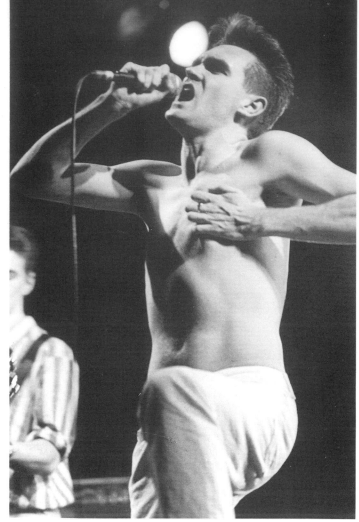

'Panic' wasn't an anti-black music song. Speaking later to the *NME*'s Danny Kelly, Johnny Marr would defend the 'Hang the blessed DJ' lyric:

"To those who took offence at the 'Burn down the disco' line, I'd say, please show me the black members of New Order. For me, personally, New Order make great disco music but there's no black people in that group. The point I'm making is that you can't just interchange the words 'black' music and 'disco' music. It makes no earthly sense."

And later, with a modicum of venom, on the subject of Mr Owen . . .

"Right then. The next time we come across that creep, he's plastered. We are not in the habit of issuing personal threats but that was such a vicious slur job that we'll kick the shit out of him. Violence is disgusting but racism's far worse and we don't deal with it."

'Panic', incidentally, was written on the day of Chernobyl and was The Smiths comment on the unassailable gulf between the reality of incidents like that and the 'I'm Your Man' state of modern pop music. That's all.

Over in America, The Smiths were evolving into a seriously huge beast. Yet still, they were without the push of a major record company. A 25-date tour saw the band both triumphant and emotionally disturbed. They didn't have the power behind them to handle such situations. Johnny Marr began to slide towards potential alcoholism, drinking a bottle of Remy Martin a night, and the band began to drift apart. They returned early and, after sending most of the major labels running for their blessed cheque books, signed to EMI. The rumours surrounding the signing were rife. The figure of one million pounds (although without knowledge of the particular contract, such a figure is totally meaningless) was constantly mentioned in the music press. As was the heavy rumour that The Smiths had already received advances for their next five albums. Personally, I didn't believe any of it.

Still, even after signing to EMI The Smiths had to maintain a further year's recording schedule with Rough Trade.

On the British Queen Is Dead Tour, The Smiths fell foul of serious crowd trouble. If we were to believe the local paper reports then we would have to accept that The Smiths were attacked by hordes of outraged royalists, which was far from the truth. At Newport Morrissey fell victim to innocent crowd over-enthusiasm and found himself dragged into the mob. This happened three quarters of the way through the set. He was shaken, slightly concussed and in no state to carry on with the show.

Speaking, again to *NME*'s Danny Kelly, Johnny Marr spoke of the snowballing effect on that tour:

"The next date, of course, was always going to be trouble. A certain element in our audience who are, basically thick, responded to what they had read over their morning cornflakes."

The tour concluded at Manchester's Free Trade Hall. A gig which saw The Smiths performing as a five-piece for the last time. Amidst accusations that Marr had used Craig Gannon to rockify the band, The Smiths dispensed with Gannon almost immediately after the curtain fell in Manchester. It would have been nice, however, if the band had informed Gannon of the decision to fire him before the rumours spread through the Mancunian underground. Not only was Gannon jettisoned with professional coldness he was, at least according to the Gannon camp, somewhat lacking in payment for the American tour and under-acknowledged for his part in the writing of The Smiths next single, 'Ask'. Yet another court case would loom from this situation although, for once, it was The Smiths who found themselves on the receiving end.

However, speaking to *Hot Press*'s George Byrne at a later date, Johnny Marr attempted to dispel the controversy surrounding Gannon: "Things were made out of that situation which we didn't intend. The real facts behind Craig's joining the group and leaving were sensationalised and fiction, really, in the British music press. The long and the short of it is that he came in to replace Andy . . . We didn't intend to have a five-piece group so we played with Craig and, in the meantime, Andy returned and we'd gotten on so well with him that we decided to continue as a five-piece . . .

"I felt that I began to get very complacent in my guitar playing and that's why we asked Craig to leave. There was no kind of animosity at all because we are still friends with him but it was just that his presence didn't do anything dramatic for the group creatively so we asked him to go."

'Ask' followed, handsomely sporting Yootha Joyce on the cover. 'Ask' was lightweight, not unattractive but hardly essential. Morrissey mused, almost comically, 'Spending long summer days indoors, writing frightening verse to a buck tooth girl in Luxembourg.'

'Ask' was an odd little record. With the help of a good deal of professional plugging, it crept quietly up to number 14 in the British chart before, equally quietly, creeping out again.

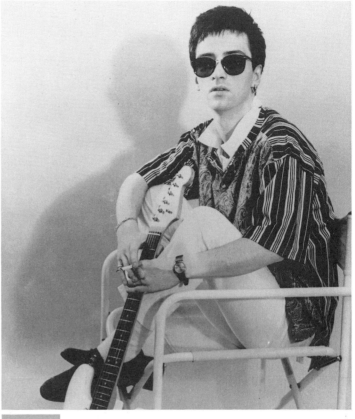

seventeen

Strangeways Here We Come

n November 1986 The Smiths were scheduled to play a huge anti-Apartheid concert with The Fall at The Royal Albert Hall. The event had to be cancelled when Johnny Marr was involved in a car crash. Apparently, Marr had been driving with his wife when he spun out of control and smashed into a brick wall. Although the car was written off, the pair escaped largely unhurt. Two days before the concert was due to take place, Marr was admitted to hospital and, although his injuries were minor, was fitted with a neck brace. Although no one could doubt the facts concerning Marr's car crash, rumour had it that Marr had other reasons for cancelling the show. Life within The Smiths was apparently strained.

Three days before the concert, and just one day before his hospital admission Johnny Marr's favourite music journalist, Nick Kent, received a phone call from Rough Trade press officer Pat Bellis (née Jo Novark).

"Johnny really wants to talk to you. He feels he has a lot to say and wants to do a serious in depth interview dealing with The Smiths current position as well as certain endeavours he's been involved in."

It was a strange way to end the year; with uncertainty all around, with a major record deal signed but held on ice for a further year, and with Andy Rourke, although recovered, standing trial for possession of heroin.

In January 1987 The Smiths' planned single release, 'You Just Haven't Earned It Yet Baby', a rather spiteful song with a catchy hookline, was switched to 'Shoplifters Of The World Unite'. The switch wasn't early enough to prevent a number of white labels leaving Rough Trade with the original A-side. 'Shoplifters' was fine though, a moody, arrogant statement that would soon see Morrissey undulating curiously on Top Of The Pops. It also provided a few snippets of absurd press. The British tabloids, always to be relied upon to turn a mild comment into a raging scandal, did just that, hilariously suggesting that The Smiths, as always, led by manic vegetarian Morrissey, were inciting the nation's kids to go shoplifting. Hardly a welcome comment on the mentality of this nation's youth who, no doubt, understood Morrissey's ambiguous lyrics rather better than the tabloids.

It was a return to form for The Smiths as a singles band, especially when the extra track on the 12 inch, 'Half A Person', was taken into account. 'Half A Person' saw Morrissey looking through the eyes of a 16-year-old runaway, complete with all the obsessive uncertainty of fandom. His ability to set his lyrics in a kind of monochrome vision, a skill he hadn't utilised since 'Hatful Of Hollow', was re-used, most welcomely.

I n February The Smiths released 'Hatful Of Hollow Part Two' or, as it is officially entitled, 'The World Won't Listen'.
A compilation album which was either, a valuable gathering of high spots, or a piece of mild exploitation on Rough Trade's behalf, depending on your point of view.

The *NME*'s Mancunian reviewer, Dave Haslam, enjoyed it. "Hey, lost in music and lost for words, you yell or purr but all you can understand is that The Smiths are special and you'll hug them to your heart . . . We're halfway to paradise, here, now, with The Smiths."

Significantly, *Melody Maker*'s Steve Sutherland was less impressed. In fact, his assault on the motivations of Morrissey's seemed interestingly savage. "It's apparent that Morrissey will STOP AT NOTHING to manufacture confrontations with the norm in order that The Smiths remain special."

Now that, I swiftly interject, is accusing The Smiths of the ultimate blandness. Controversy for controversy's sake, is the weakest, most pathetic form of art. Sutherland continued: "But lately, in his perpetual need to IRRITATE, to keep The Smiths APART, Morrissey's taken on a cosmetic political stance which could be a dark mirror intentionally reflecting the pathetic propaganda that pollutes this nation just prior to a general election."

Poor Morrissey. All he thought he had done was to assemble a collection of his favourite songs.

Sutherland finishes: " . . . it's you, The Smiths fan, who Morrissey's mocking. A career in outrage is a fine place to be but some jokes just aren't funny any more."

Ah yes. The old Smiths paradox begins to rear its naturally ugly head once more. Scandal, bitterness, insincerity, money, obsession, all furthered by, at times, blind fan adoration. The album's title is the true irony. It should have been called, 'The World Is Only Too Keen To Listen.'

It is also only too keen to buy and, just two months after the release of 'The World Won't Listen', Rough Trade were forced into the position of issuing yet another Smiths compilation album, this time a double album, on to the English record racks. Initially planned to help educate new American listeners, 'Louder Than Bombs' proved to be a mish mash of 'The World Won't Listen', 'Hatful Of Hollow' and the forthcoming single,

'Sheila Take A Bow'/'Is It Really So Strange' and 'Sweet And Tender Hooligan'. I find it a rather jagged compilation, certainly devoid of the warmth and innocence of 'Hatful Of Hollow'. To avoid the album selling for ludicrous amounts on import, Rough Trade took the decision to issue it in Britain.

As 'Sheila Take A Bow' climbed on to the playlists, rumours about a split in the Smiths camp again reached fever pitch. Although a number of rather insincere sounding press interviews gave no hint of any rift (in fact they seemed to make a point of stating the reverse, itself a suspicious fact) it was said that Morrissey had taken exception to Marr's increasing amount of non-Smiths activities. His recent work with Bryan Ferry was reported to have caused particular upset to Morrissey.

'Sheila Take A Bow' was not a good single. It lacked co-ordination and Morrissey's ability to surprise people with words, seemed strangely lacking. As the *NME* would later note, "A TV appearance to promote 'Sheila' pours nitroglycerine on the flames (of the 'split rumours'). Marr sneers through on auto while Morrissey flails, unsure, agitated, scared near to panic. The conclusion is obvious and unavoidable. This is a band at the end of their tether."

But what about poor EMI? A phone call to the company produced nothing but a (too) hasty denial that anything was wrong in Smithdom. Work on the final Rough Trade album, intriguingly, mysteriously entitled 'Strangeways Here We Come' had been completed and the band were, apparently, leading separate lives.

On July 23, Mancunian freelance journalist Steven Kingston visited the Rough Trade offices to interview Morrissey. Before the meeting took place, Pat Bellis took Kingston to one side to enquire just who it was who was spreading the 'split' rumours in Manchester. Bellis was adamant that there was no truth at all in these stories. In the unpublished conclusion to the interview, Kingston tentatively broached the subject.

Kingston: "There have been some quite strong rumours flying around Manchester that the band are about to split up . . . "

Morrissey: "I'm not really sure where they came from. To begin with I find it very interesting. I'd be very interested to hear what the next rumour is . . . but I don't really have anything to say. Yes, the band's very happy – we all think the next LP is the best record we've ever made."

The rumours were now more than just loud, they were deafening. It didn't help that The Smiths video for the gorgeously maudlin 'Girlfriend In A Coma' featured the sad impassioned face of Morrissey and only Morrissey. The single itself was tragic to almost comic proportions. "I think it's a very jolly pop record really," quoth Morrissey to a totally baffled tabloid press.

Meanwhile, back in Manchester, The Smiths' favourite local photographer Steve Wright (who shot the Salford Lads Club picture on the inside gatefold of 'The Queen Is Dead') was duly dispatched to a grubby street in Salford to snap a Strangeways road sign. The album was imminent but, just six days after the Bellis and Morrissey denial, The Smiths really did split up. When it happened, it became comic. The music press scrambled around, at times rather pathetically, to grasp hold of the truth. The truth, however, varied immensely depending on which source they approached. Although it seems pointless to reiterate the immense journalistic gaffs that screamed from most music papers (Smiths tour dates etc) it was their beloved *NME* who broke the official story first. It seemed that Johnny Marr had left the group and a statement issued on behalf of the band ran thus: "The Smiths announce that Johnny Marr has left the group. However, they would like

to confirm that other guitarists are being considered to replace him. It must be stressed that the concept of The Smiths will remain the same and the group will continue to promote their forthcoming single and album releases and are eager to plan live dates once a new guitarist has been selected.''

Morrissey asked his old friend, former Easterhouse guitarist Ivor Perry (then with the infant Cradle) to work with him with the possibility of Perry becoming Marr's replacement. Reports that Morrissey was working with Craig Gannon once more couldn't have been further from the truth as the Gannon legal action continued. However, it was easy to see where the confusion lay, for Gannon was also a member of The Cradle.

On August 8 Johnny Marr, who wasn't consulted about the above communication, issued this reply to the *NME*: "There is nothing approaching acrimony between myself and the other members of the band. I've known them all a long time and I love 'em . . . The major reason for me going was simply that what I want to do musically, there is just not scope for in The Smiths. I've already recorded some stuff and it's gone really well. If the rest of it goes as well then there's every chance I'll be forming a permanent group. But I definitely want some live dates set up by the new year at the latest. I don't want to get over-emotional about this but I really am massively proud of the things that The Smiths have done and achieved and from that point of view, of course, it's all really sad . . . But in the final analysis, the thing that used to make me happy was making me miserable, so I just had to get out.''

Now all this hinted, I'm sure you will agree, that the split had been brewing, indeed planned for some time. Both Marr and Morrissey were instantly involved in fairly advanced post-Morrissey/Marr/Smiths activities. Once again we ask, what of poor old EMI?

EMI A&R boss Nick Gatfield could shed little light on the situation: "It's all up in the air at the moment, we are not sure what is going to happen. Essentially, we now have two acts for the price of one.''

Now where have we heard that one before? Certainly EMI were not aware of the situation when, in every wine bar in every trendy quarter in every town, Smiths fans knew, with confident certainty, the truth.

As the sessions with Ivor Perry broke down, the rumours surrounding Johnny Marr's replacement became particularly colourful; the reclusive Roddy Frame and unreclusive Johnny Thunders, to name but two. Frame had actually been approached but, sensibly perhaps, declined to involve himself.

Within the ranks of the music press, there seemed to be a genuine grief at the split and the band's loyal followers responded accordingly, filling the letter pages with tearful, doleful sentiment. Personally, I regarded it as a good thing. Whatever was to happen next, The Smiths would be preserved forever, within the highlights of their brief existence. They wouldn't mellow into CD middle age, at least not as the original band.

Then a strange thing happened. As the search for a suitable guitarist proved fruitless, it appeared that The Smiths would not be carrying on as a unit. There was always going to be heavy legal problems surrounding the continued use of the name The Smiths anyway, and the problems in furthering the band became unassailable. Joyce and Rourke would not be working with Morrissey. Sensationally, The Smiths would not be carrying on as a band at all. This was swiftly followed by the report that Rourke and Joyce would be working with Johnny Marr. Suddenly, it was Morrissey who became the outcast. His confident appearances in the music press just didn't ring true. It seemed that Morrissey was asserting his power over the media in order to make a point. It seemed forced and very odd. All this preceded the release of the last album The Smiths will ever make, 'Strangeways, Here We Come'.

So on September 12 1987, an album was issued by an extinct pop group. It could have been a glorious finale, but it wasn't. Most of the reviews admitted slight disappointment before bowing to the fact that a flawed Smiths album was still better than anything else on offer. This may well have been the case in September 1987 but I thought most reviewers were scared to dive in and uncover the record's moments of uncoordinated parody for fear of being trampled to death by hordes of rampant Smiths devotees.

'Strangeways Here We Come' was a good but heavily flawed record. The sardonic arrogance and irresistible irony that flavoured 'The Queen Is Dead' was still there, but only in fleeting moments. The opening line, 'I am the ghost of troubled Joe,' (from 'A Rush And A Push And The Land Is Ours') almost gave the game away. Was Morrissey distancing himself from the proceedings? Obviously not, as he clearly stated that he thought 'Strangeways, Here We Come' was the best work that The Smiths had ever done. 'Stop Me If You Think You've Heard This One Before' was an all too obvious attack on the band's critics and 'Death Of A Disco Dancer' was pure

Pink Floyd. Pastiche or not, 'Disco Dancer' lived in the kind of predictability that Morrissey, if he were to be truly distanced from The Smiths, would denounce fervently. Still, the album's redeeming features made it worthwhile trekking through the odd patch of lacklustre mud. 'I Started Something I Couldn't Finish' was a cute and solid pop song with Morrissey growling determinedly in comical self analysis. 'Typical me, typical me, typical me,' he mused, as typically, all around him, the band were beginning to crumble. I have this corny vision of Morrissey standing in the post-apocalyptic rubble, with his hand on his heart, desperately trying to finish a lyric before being eaten by a mutant.

The best moment on 'Strangeways, Here We Come' was, strangely, the most obvious statement Morrissey had ever made in a lyric, 'Paint A Vulgar Picture' offered no new insights to the tacky edge of such a subject, but it did sound as though he had finally decided to cast away all the ambiguity of his writing and head, simplistically, for the jugular.

'At the record company party, on their hands a dead star at last, the sycophantic slags all say, "I knew him best and I knew him well".'

Morrissey also took a swipe, albeit briefly, at fan adoration. 'I walked a pace behind you at the soundcheck, you're just the same as I' and, of course, marketing ploys . . . 'Re-issue, repackage, repackage, double pack with a photograph, extra track with a tacky badge.'

That may be Morrissey ridiculing the entire music business system, cheapening it even, but, in doing so, he was merely ridiculing himself. For all their ethics, The Smiths were as guilty as any band in the history of popular music when talking about marketing ploys and promotional tactics.

The most alarming thing about 'Strangeways, Here We Come', apart from the three or four below par tracks, was the cold, cynical undertone that darkens the album's entire lyric. No more the naivety of the 'Hatful Of Hollow' collection or the word play whimsy of 'The Queen Is Dead'. Beneath the crust of 'Strangeways' lies an utterly defensive Morrissey. Understandable maybe, but noticeably lacking in warmth.

Even now, as I type in retrospect, 'Strangeways, Here We Come' plays on the hi-fi, filling the room with Morrissey's unbecoming bitterness. Ironically, 'Strangeways, Here We Come' was the first truly depressing record the band ever made.

eighteen

'I know it's over'

roke, bitter, confused, wary. Hardly appropriate words for pop musicians who have spent five years as a fundamental part of one of Britain's most successful rock bands. Yet, in October 1987, in the post 'Strangeways' scramble, Andy Rourke, Mike Joyce and, to a lesser extent, Craig Gannon, were beginning to realise that life after The Smiths would be like starting over again. They had their name, their skill and their hunger. Unfortunately, as The Smiths were always, in effect, just Morrissey and Marr, they didn't have the money. Morrissey and Marr, on the other hand, were preparing to move into the international first division. Morrissey engaged the considerable managerial talents of Gail Colson, who also, significantly, manages Peter Gabriel. Johnny Marr guested with everyone from A Certain Ratio to Bryan Ferry, finally finishing 1987, somewhat bizarrely, as a member of The Pretenders.

Rourke, Gannon and Joyce played with The Fall's Brix Smith, as The Adult Net, performing a one-off gig at London's ICA. However, despite a flurry of good reviews, the ex-Smiths trio decided not to become serious part-time members of the unit, much to the consternation of Brix.

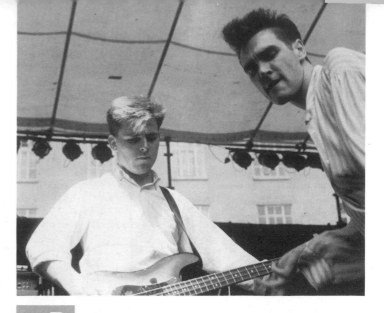

R ough Trade released two more singles from 'Strangeways, Here We Come'. 'I Started Something I Couldn't Finish' and 'Last Night I Dreamt That Somebody Loved Me'. The former producing a hilarious video with Morrissey and assorted bespectacled lookalikes riding pushbikes through Salford.

And, of course, we all set our videos to record the much hyped South Bank Show special on The Smiths. We expected it to somehow embrace the undisputed magic of the band. Unfortunately, it managed to produce quite the reverse. In the words of a close associate of mine, and professional northerner to boot, "It was just a platform for a load of posey, irrelevant southerners to use The Smiths to gain publicity." I can't better that. It certainly looked that way. Oh how we laughed at Nick Kent, who may well be the greatest rock journalist who ever lived, but he epitomised every cliché in the 'Oh yeah man, we was stoned' book. It had little to do with The Smiths.

By this time Morrissey, never one to gather moss, had begun working in earnest with producer Steven Street and Durutti Column guitarist Vini Reilly. Photographer Steve Wright was sent to Warrington to take a shot of George Formby's gravestone which was to feature on Morrissey's début EMI single sleeve. (The idea was later scrapped). Suddenly it all began to look hopeful again. From the unholy mess that was the latter-day Smiths, to a period of hope and promise. Once more we could look forward with anticipatory glee. What would Morrissey's solo stuff sound like? Would he tour with a band? Would Marr get a band together? Would either of them reach compact disc standard international stardom and, if they did, would they soften into insignificance or would they, could they, remain essential and innovative?

Occasionally, we could look back to The Smiths. A unique band. A genuinely pure concept that just couldn't possibly last. It would have been nice though. Yes, The Smiths. Very nice, very nice, very nice . . . but maybe in the next world.

SINGLES

Hand in Glove/Handsome Devil
Rough Trade RT 132. Released May 1983

This Charming Man/Jeane
Rough Trade RT 136. Released November 1983.

This Charming Man (Manchester)/This Charming Man (London)/Accept Yourself/Wonderful Woman
Rough Trade RT 136 12″. Released November 1983.

This Charming Man New York/This Charming Man (instrumental) (Now deleted but may be found in large stores).
Rough Trade 136. Released December 1983.

What Difference Does It Make/Back To The Old House
Rough Trade RT 146. Released January 1984.

What Difference Does It Make/Back To The Old House/These Things Take Time
Rough Trade RT 146 12″. Released February 1984.

Hand In Glove/I Don't Owe You Anything (Sandie Shaw with The Smiths)
Rough Trade RT 130. Released April 1984.

Hand In Glove/I Don't Owe You Anything/Jeane (Sandie Shaw with The Smiths)
Rough Trade RT 130 12″. Released April 1984.

Heaven Knows I'm Miserable Now/Suffer Little Children
Rough Trade RT 156. Released May 1984.

Heaven Knows I'm Miserable Now/Suffer Little Children/Girl Afraid
Rough Trade RT 156 12″. Released May 1984.

William It Was Really Nothing/Please Please Please Let Me Get What I Want
Rough Trade RT 166. Released August 1984.

William It Was Really Nothing/Please Please Please Let Me Get What I Want/How Soon Is Now
Rough Trade RT 166 12″. Released August 1984.

How Soon is Now/Well I Wonder
Rough Trade RT 176. Released February 1985.

How Soon Is Now/Well I Wonder/Oscillate Wildly
Rough Trade RT 176 12″. Released February 1985.

Shakespeare's Sister/What She Said
Rough Trade RT 181. Released March 1985.

Shakespeare's Sister/What She Said/Stretch Out And Wait
Rough Trade RT 181 12″. Released March 1985.

That Joke Isn't Funny Anymore/Meat Is Murder (live)
Rough Trade RT 186. Released July 1985.

That Joke Isn't Funny Anymore/Nowhere Fast (live)/Stretch Out And Wait (live)/Shakespeare's Sister (live)/Meat Is Murder (live)
Rough Trade RT 186 12″. Released July 1985.

Big Mouth Strikes Again/Money Changes Everything.
Rough Trade RT 192. Released May 1986.
Big Mouth Strikes Again/Money Changes Everything/Unloveable.
Rough Trade. RT 192. 12 inch. Released May 1986.
Panic/Vicar In A Tutu.
Rough Trade. RT 193. Released July 1986.
Panic/Vicar In A Tutu/The Draize Train.
Rough Trade. RTT 193. 12 inch. Released July 1986.
Ask/Cemetery Gates.
Rough Trade. RT 194. Released October 1986.
Ask/Cemetery Gates/Golden Lights.
Rough Trade. RTT 194. 12 inch. Released October 1986.
Ask/Cemetery Gates/Golden Lights.
Rough Trade. RTT 194c. Cassingle. Released October 1986.
Shoplifters Of The World Unite/Half A Person.
Rough Trade. RT 195. Released January 1987.
Shoplifters Of The World Unite/Half A Person/London.
Rough Trade RTT 195. 12 inch. Released January 1987.
You Just Haven't Earned It Yet Baby/Half A Person/ London.
(Mispress 12 inch. January 1987).
Sheila Take A Bow/Is It Really So Strange.
Rough Trade. RT 196. Released April 1987.
Sheila Take A Bow/Is It Really So Strange/Sweet And Tender Hooligan.
Rough Trade. RTT 196. 12 inch. Released April 1987.
Girlfriend In A Coma/I Keep Mine Hidden.
Rough Trade. RT 197. Released July 1987.
Girlfriend In A Coma/I Keep Mine Hidden/Work Is A Four Letter Word.
Rough Trade. RTT 197. 12 inch. Released July 1987.
I Started Something I Couldn't Finish/Pretty Girls Make Graves.
Rough Trade. RT 198. Released October 1987.
I Started Something I Couldn't Finish/Pretty Girls Make Graves/Some Girls Are Bigger Than Others.
Rough Trade. RTT 198. 12 inch. Released October 1987.
Last Night I Dreamt That Somebody Loved Me/ Rusholme Ruffians.
Rough Trade. RT 200. Released December 1987.
Last Night I Dreamt That Somebody Loved Me/ Rusholme Ruffians/Nowhere Fast.
Rough Trade. RTT 200. 12 inch. Released December 1987.

ALBUMS

THE SMITHS
Rough Trade ROUGH 61
Released February 1984.
Reel Around The Fountain/You've Got Everything Now/
Miserable Lie/Pretty Girls Make Graves/The Hand That
Rocks The Cradle/Still Ill/Hand In Glove/What Difference
Does It Make/I Don't Owe You Anything/Suffer Little
Children.

HATFUL OF HOLLOW
Rough Trade ROUGH 76
Released November 1984
William It Was Really Nothing/What Difference Does It
Make/These Things Take Time/This Charming Man/How
Soon Is Now/Handsome Devil/Hand In Glove/Still Ill/
Heaven Knows I'm Miserable Now/This Night Has Opened
My Eyes/You've Got Everything Now/Accept Yourself/Girl
Afraid/Back To The Old House/Reel Around The Fountain/
Please Please Please Let Me Get What I Want.

MEAT IS MURDER
Rough Trade ROUGH 81
Released February 1985
The Headmaster Ritual/Rusholme Ruffians/I Want The
One I Can't Have/What She Said/That Joke Isn't Funny
Anymore/Nowhcrc Fast/Well I Wonder/Barbarism Begins
At Home/Meat Is Murder.
(Also available as Compact Disc: Rough Trade ROUGH
CD 81, released April 1985.)

THE QUEEN IS DEAD
Rough Trade. ROUGH 96.
Released June 1986.
The Queen Is Dead/Frankly Mr Shankly/I Know It's Over/
Never Had No One Ever/Cemetery Gates/ Big Mouth
Strikes Again/The Boy With The Thorn In His Side/Vicar
In A Tutu/There Is A Light That Never Goes Out/Some
Girls Are Bigger Than Others.

THE WORLD WON'T LISTEN
Rough Trade. ROUGH 101.
Released March 1987.
Panic/Ask/London/Big Mouth Strikes Again/
Shakespeare's Sister/There Is A Light That Never Goes
Out/Shoplifters Of The World Unite/The Boy With The
Thorn In His Side/Asleep/Unloveable/Half A Person/
Stretch Out And Wait/That Joke Isn't Funny Anymore/
Oscillate Wildly/You Just Haven't Earned It Yet, Baby/
Rubber Ring.

LOUDER THAN BOMBS
Sire. 9 25568-1. (Double US Import).
Released April 1987.

STRANGEWAYS HERE WE COME
Rough Trade. ROUGH 106.
Released September 1987.
A Rush And A Push And The Land Is Ours/I Started
Something I Couldn't Finish/Death Of A Disco Dancer/
Girlfriend In A Coma/Stop Me If You've Heard This One
Before/Last Night I Dreamt That Somebody Loved Me/
Unhappy Birthday/Paint A Vulgar Picture/Death At One's
Elbow/I Won't Share You.

COMPACT DISCS

MEAT IS MURDER
Rough Trade ROUGH C.D.81. Released April 1985.

HATFUL OF HOLLOW
Rough Trade ROUGH C.D.76. Released December 1985.

THE QUEEN IS DEAD
Rough Trade. ROUGH C.D.96. Released June 1986.

THE SMITHS
Rough Trade. ROUGH. C.D.61. Released October 1986.

THE WORLD WON'T LISTEN
Rough Trade. ROUGH. C.D.101. Released March 1987.

STRANGEWAYS HERE WE COME
Rough Trade. ROUGH. C.D.106. Released October 1987.

(There are a number of Smiths bootleg recordings
currently in circulation, mainly 'live' albums from
The Smiths British tours.
The quality of these is appalling and they are never
worth the inflated price).